Cabin Trunks
& Far Horizons

"GRANDPA"
Surgeon Rear Admiral ARNOLD ASHWORTH POMFRET R.N. CBE
OBE MB ChB DO(Oxon) DOMS
b. 1st June 1900, d. 3rd April 1984
*This photograph was taken just after his investiture as a Companion of the
Order of the Bath in 1957 by Her Majesty Queen Elizabeth II*

Cabin Trunks
& Far Horizons

by
Carlene Pomfret

MM Productions Ltd

Published 1991 in Great Britain by
MM Productions Ltd
8b East Street
Ware
Hertfordshire
SG12 9HJ
(Telephone: 0920 466003, Fax: 0920 462267)

British Library Cataloguing in Publication Data

Pomfret, Carlene
    Cabin trunks and far horizons
    I. Title
    910.4092

ISBN 0 9517685 06

Typeset in Palatino 10/11pt by Area Graphics Ltd.
Printed in Great Britain by Billings Book Plan Limited, Worcester.

Contents

Henry Duke of Gloucester ═══

Knight of the Most Noble Order of the Garter, Grand Prior in the British Realm of the Venerable Order of the Hospital of St John of Jerusalem, to

Surgeon Rear-Admiral Arnold Ashworth Pomfret,
C.B·O.B.E·M.B·Ch·B·Q.H.S.
Greeting.

Whereas Her Majesty the Queen, the Sovereign Head in the British Realm of the Venerable Order of the Hospital of St John of Jerusalem, has thought fit to sanction your appointment as a Commander in the said Venerable Order.

Now therefore I, by these presents, in the name and by the authority of Her Majesty, do grant unto you the Dignity of a Commander in the said Venerable Order and I do hereby authorize you to have, hold and enjoy the said Dignity as a Commander of the aforesaid Order, together with all and singular the privileges thereunto belonging, or appertaining.

Given at St John's Gate under the Signature of His Royal Highness The Grand Prior, and the Seal of the said Venerable Order this Twenty-second day of May One thousand Nine hundred and Fifty-seven in the Sixth year of Her Majesty's Reign.

By the Grand Prior's Command

Henry R. Pownall
Chancellor.

Grant of the Dignity of a Commander of the Venerable Order of the Hospital of St John of Jerusalem to
Surgeon Rear-Admiral Arnold Ashworth Pomfret, C.B., O.B.E., M.B., Ch.B., Q.H.S. Reg. № 26421.

Preface

How is it that I came to write this book at all? Who could be interested in my life? I've performed no great exploit, invented nothing, achieved no particular success in any academic or practical field.

But I have led a most interesting life as the wife of a Naval Officer and as such have circumnavigated the globe more than two and a half times over. My two daughters, Jill and Jocelyn were with me on virtually all of these travels and know most of the details. My son John arrived much later though and wasn't as fortunate as his sisters in seeing so much of the world in my company. But it's their children, my grandchildren, who have persistently pressed me for details of all my experiences. Now, I even have some great grandchildren. No doubt they too will want to know about their distant ancestor's experiences spanning two world wars, and covering almost a complete century. Also, my great friend Allie has urged me to put everything down for posterity. So, here it is. I hope you find it interesting, enlightening and amusing too. My lifetime has been a fascinating one. Perhaps my story about it will fascinate you!

As I've written primarily for my grandchildren's eyes, it seemed natural to refer to my husband Arnold, who passed over seven years ago, as they did. As "Grandpa". Others will have to make the necessary adjustment to "Daddy" etc as they find appropriate.

Travel with us and share our emotions and tales of intrigue and excitement across 4 continents.

January 1991   *Carlene Pomfret*

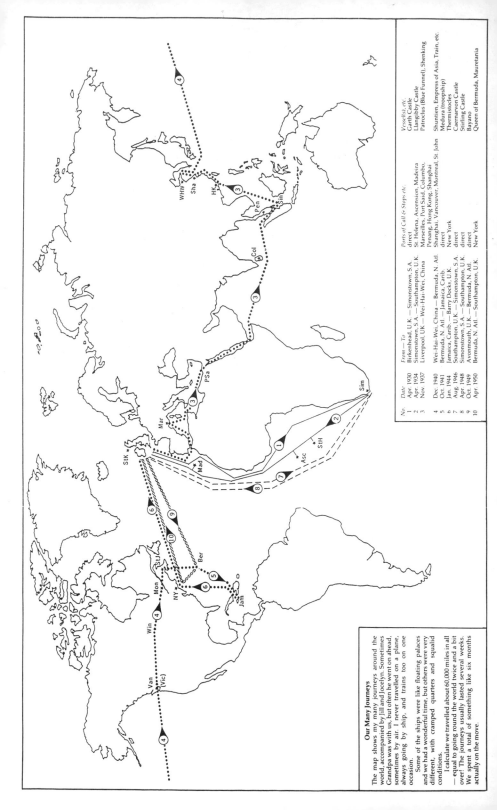

Our Many Journeys

The map shows my many journeys around the world, accompanied by Jill and Jocelyn. Sometimes Grandpa was with us, but often he went on ahead, sometimes by air. I never travelled on a plane, always going by ship, and trains too on one occasion.

Some of the ships were like floating palaces and we had a wonderful time, but others were very different, with cramped quarters and squalid conditions.

I calculate we travelled about 60,000 miles in all — equal to going round the world twice and a bit over! The journeys usually lasted several weeks. We spent a total of something like six months actually on the move.

No.	Date	From — To	Ports of Call & Stops, etc.	Vessel(s), etc.
1	Apr. 1930	Birkenhead, U.K. — Simonstown, S.A.	direct	Garth Castle
2	Apr. 1934	Simonstown, S.A. — Southampton, U.K.	St Helena, Ascension, Madeira	Llangibby Castle
3	Nov. 1937	Liverpool, U.K. — Wei-Hai-Wei, China	Marseilles, Port Said, Columbo, Penang, Hong Kong, Shanghai	Patroclus (Blue Funnel), Shenking
4	Dec. 1940	Wei-Hai-Wei, China — Bermuda, N. Atl.	Shanghai, Vancouver, Montreal, St John	Shuntien, Empress of Asia, Train, etc.
5	Oct. 1941	Bermuda, N. Atl. — Jamaica, Carib.	direct	Medura (troopship)
6	Jan. 1944	Jamaica, Carib. — Barry Docks, U.K.	New York	Thermistocles
7	Aug. 1946	Southampton, U.K. — Simonstown, S.A.	direct	Caernarvon Castle
8	Apr. 1948	Simonstown, S.A. — Southampton, U.K.	direct	Stirling Castle
9	Oct. 1949	Avonmouth, U.K. — Bermuda, N. Atl.	direct	Bayano
10	Apr. 1950	Bermuda, N. Atl. — Southampton, U.K.	New York	Queen of Bermuda, Mauretania

CHAPTER 1
Engaged and Married

Our betrothal, wedding and honeymoon

I met Arnold Pomfret, a dashing young doctor at a house party the Bramelds were giving over Christmas 1926. When all the guests had left he rushed me into the drawing room and kissed me under the mistletoe. I fell in love with him on the spot. He was trying out General Practice, having been in the Navy before, but finding it didn't suit him at all, had applied to rejoin the Navy and had been accepted. I didn't know at the time that he was already committed to this course of action, and was only working out the last four months of the Retford practice before going back to sea.

I was terribly sad and miserable when Grandpa went back into the Navy, going off in H.M.S. Endeavour to the Red Sea. He was actually away for about a year, apart from six weeks leave when he always rushed to Mansfield to see me.

Mother and I were still living in Mansfield when, one afternoon, up drove Arthur Philipson and Grandpa on a motorbike and sidecar. Surprised but delighted to see them, I readily accepted when they suggested we go for a spin. I climbed into the sidecar, Grandpa perched behind Arthur and off we went to Sherwood Forest. I had no idea how exciting the result of this trip would be, or how far reaching the consequences. During this afternoon, Arthur made himself scarce, and Grandpa and I, wandering between the trees, found ourselves close to the Major Oak. This centuries old tree is a popular attraction and is the

subject of scores of legends. Well, for me it got another that day;
one I'm never likely to forget, for there it was that he proposed to
me and I accepted. We got the engagement ring next day in
Nottingham. Actually we'd been unoffically engaged for some
weeks, mother being quite vexed about our relationship, saying
she was sure that it wouldn't work out. When it became official
though, she resigned herself to the inevitable, even though she
may have harboured other ideas that were now definitely "off"
The Mansfield house was given up in November of 1927, and we
went to live with friends for a while. During this time I managed
to get scarlet fever, which had some special relevance just after
Jill was born about two years later.

During one of his leaves Grandpa persuaded me to go and
live with his Aunt Grayson in Rochdale, where she lived in
Drake Street with her husband and two children, Allie and
Jackie. I lived there with Grandpa's Aunt, her husband and their
two children for four months, a wonderful happy time. Allie,
their thirteen year old daughter, was to be one of my
bridesmaids, although Jackie, being only eight was considered
too young to come to the wedding! Jackie always reminded me of
that lovable but tiresome character William of the "Just William"
stories, popular books in those days and for many years to come.

I was treated as one of the family and we all grew very fond
of each other, Aunt Grayson being great company for me. We
went shopping to Manchester together many times, getting my
bridal veil from Kendal Milnes as well as the satin for my gown.
Fortunately, I realised that the universal "up to the   e"
fashions so popular then were really very ugly. Just look at my
wedding photo to see what I mean. I decided that I wouldn't look
so absurd on my big day and so I designed my own dress in a
style that would bear scrutiny for years to come. How wise I was.

Uncle Grayson was an industrial chemist, a man of many
talents, one being playing chess for England, and a member of
the Manchester Chess Club, writing books and doing his own
illustrations. He played chess publicly, memorising half a dozen
boards and then playing his opponents from memory. My
twentieth birthday was a lovely day. Uncle Grayson gave me
twenty small presents, leaving one on each step of the stairs. As I
came down that morning I had the excitement of picking up and
unwrapping each one in turn! I cherish the memory of this and
many other happy occasions in that house.

I have one snap that shows Jackie with his much loved
meccano set, always a bone of contention as he'd leave bits of it
all over the place complaining loudly if any of it went missing or

got trodden on. He was ever to be found creating elaborate and ingenious constructions. One of these I remember especially well. Aunt Grayson and I arrived back in the early evening from a shopping trip to Manchester, where we had also taken in a matinee of "Hit the Deck". Whacked out, we were longing for a cup of tea. Opening the drawing room door the sight that met our eyes had to be seen to be believed. Uncle Grayson was on his knees at one end of the vast floor, engrossed in two tyres and half the insides of "Felix", his car, with oil cans and tools strewn all around on the carpet. At the other end of this enormous room Jackie lay on his stomach inspecting a huge tower of meccano nearing completion. Their startled faces stared up at us in disbelief and dismay. We had been well out of the way for the day, and they were making the most of it. Time had obviously meant nothing, and we hadn't been expected for some hours yet. Aunt just stood there silently for a few ominous seconds, before becoming a red headed, five foot tall fury, her light blue eyes flashing as she let fly with a tirade that would have done justice to any sergeant on a parade ground. No bad language, mind you, but what she said got that room cleared in ten minutes flat, with only an odd oily rag and a few nuts and screws left under the rug to show they'd ever been there at all. I crept off to the kitchen to have a good laugh. Jackie and Uncle sensibly made themselves scarce for several hours to give the dust time to settle! Traces of oil on the carpet only served to further the fury. Next day Mrs Plaice, their daily woman, had difficulty trying to remove the stains, not having the benefit of detergents. There was only soap, a solid block of compressed scouring powder like Vim, called "Monkey Brand", and a powder called "Panshine". Quite frequently Aunt and I went to the best shows, which luckily often opened in Manchester. Never again though did we come home to a scene like that. I'll always remember the look of shock on those upturned faces.

Jackie's now a brilliant physicist, having written many books, but he's still just as lovable, whilst Alice became a talented artist. In the days I'm referring to, though, just before my marriage, they were a pair of real pests, delightful pests it's true, and I loved them, but unpredictable and clumsy. The night before my wedding I'd got all my beautiful regalia draped around my bedroom on hangers, over the backs of chairs etc with my white satin slippers on a chair near the door. Molly, another of Grandpa's cousins, was sharing a big bed with me for that night as the house was so full. Early the next morning, my big day, we were wide-awake talking about all the exciting events ahead when the door burst open. In charged Allie without looking where she was going to crash into the chair and, to my horror, finishing up in a heap of white satin and net. Molly and I let out loud yelps and, of course, Allie was, "so sorry". My precious shoes were knocked flying and had to be sought on hands and knees from under the bed. This was the sort of activity one could always expect from either of those two! I wonder if Mollie remembers the episode.

A month before my own wedding I witnessed a highly entertaining incident nearby, which greatly diverted us all. A charming couple lived next door, with whom we had all become great friends, a Dr. Emmett, who had qualified with Grandpa, and his wife. Just beyond the Emmett's was a Methodist Chapel, where a wedding took place most Saturdays. I much enjoyed watching the many weddings. Standing in a side window I could see everyone, including the bride and her retinue, arriving and leaving. One Saturday a party arrived and went in. Whilst I was waiting to see them leave after the ceremony was over, an ambulance suddenly dashed up, stopping outside the Church. Thinking a guest had been taken ill I was agog! Dr. Emmett rushed out and got into it with someone on a stretcher. I just couldn't wait to relay all this to Aunt Grayson. We waited expectantly for about an hour. Dr. Emmett eventually walked in convulsed with laughter. He'd just come from the hospital where the bride was now sitting up with a fine son! It amused us as the wedding was a white, full regalia, veil and everything affair! I know these days some people can run it pretty fine, but this was 1928, and nothing could have been "finer" than that!

Aunt Grayson must have been about 40 in those days, and the four months I spent with them hold treasured memories for me, not only of tennis parties, picnics and visits to the theatre but also going on many exciting shopping expeditions.

One unforgettable incident was when Aunt G and I decided to bath the cat. Black with a white vest, he was called Nigger, but doubtless that wouldn't be allowed in these days, but then the world has gone mad since 1928. We'd noticed his vest had become quite undistinguishable from the rest of him as he never seemed to wash himself. The grime and dirt in the towns then was quite unbelievable with no smoke free zones or smokeless fuel. An old enamel bath, filled with tepid water was made ready on towels and mats spread in the middle of the very big kitchen floor, with a packet of Lux to one side. Then we set out to catch him, but he must have had some uncanny feeling that he might be involved in all these preparations and had fled. We called, coaxed and threatened. Every room of the very large three storey house was searched. Luckily we'd closed the cellar door, but we still couldn't find him anywhere. Eventually, found in hiding behind a chest of drawers, he was dragged out and carried downstairs. Although we knew the operation wouldn't be exactly easy, we had no idea of the party that would follow. Gingerly he was lowered into the warm water. He sprang to life on the instant fighting us tooth to claw, shrieking, hissing, biting and threshing about so wildly that we had a full time job just holding him down never mind washing him. Having got so far we couldn't give in though, and holding on grimly we somehow got him soaped, well and truly covered in bubbles. Then he made a last great struggle, leaping from our grasp to streak out of the kitchen window. Having been gone for three whole days, he finally made a very tentative appearance but just as completely scruffy as he had been before we started, in fact if anything rather worse! Thinking about it, Aunt and I concluded that this hadn't been one of our better ideas.

I was married in 1928 from Aunt Grayson's house on Drake Street where I was still living. After months of shopping, dress

My Wedding Day, July 30th 1928

| John Pomfret *groom's father* | Allie Grayson *bridesmaid* | Maggie Blundstone *bride's mother* | The Bride & Groom | John Grayson *groom's uncle* | Margot Blundstone *bride's sister* |

Mrs. Blundstone

requests the pleasure of
the company of

....

at the marriage of her daughter

Carline,

with

Surgeon Lieut.Arnold Ashworth Pomfret,
at the Rochdale Parish Church,   R.N.

on Monday, July 30th, 1928,

at 11 a.m.,

and afterwards at Balderstone Hall.

169 Drake Street.   R.S.V.P.
Rochdale.   before July 15th.

fittings and other preparations that most important and exciting day of my life, July 30th 1928, arrived at long last. I was to marry Arnold Pomfret at 11.00 a.m. in the Parish Church in Rochdale. The flowers had arrived, the weather was wonderful, and I stood inspecting myself in the long swivel mirror. I confess I was extremely satisfied with what I saw. A perfectly fitting shimmering white satin gown, slightly raised at the front to show a contrasting, delicate shell pink lining, together with veil and orange blossom arranged in contemporary fashion. Carrying my bouquet of lovely Regale lilies which encased me in a cloud of their heady perfume, I emerged through the front door onto the short flight of steps down to street level. A magical moment. The photographers had a field day, calling out, "This way. This way, please", and "Look over here, please".

Looking back sixty-one years, can the radiant girl I see in those photos really be me, I wonder? Can she have become what I now see, when, reluctantly, I glance in my mirror? Watching today's brides on their special day I know they're feeling just as I did. Or are they? Unlike me, most of them have probably had years of experience of living together, and a succession of "meaningful relationships", which I'd have thought would have wiped some of the "gilt off the gingerbread". Without condemning modern ideas, it seems to me rather like unwrapping your presents before Xmas. I'm a very firm believer in marriage, — and divorce too, if things turn out badly. Any children should be considered first of course. But, to my mind, it's much better for a child to be brought up by a sole happy, loving parent than by two incompatible, nagging people who detest the sight of each other.

Such unpleasant thoughts were far from my mind as I set out on the short journey to the Parish Church on my day of days. Proceeding out of Church arm in arm with my very handsome partner, I made sure my gold wedding ring was quite visible to the many cameras clicking away. The rest of the day had a haze like quality, although I recall it well. Some forty guests attended the delightfully formal reception at Balderstone Hall, just outside Rochdale. As usual bride and groom had pride of place at the top of the T shaped table, with the cake displayed before them. Many relatives and friends had come from far away, three of my closest school friends driving up in a little Austin car all the way from Mansfield. Most of Grandpa's relatives I'd never met before. I had such a splendid time I was sorry to leave for my honeymoon, catching a train for Liverpool en route to the Isle of Man. Staying at a Liverpool hotel overnight we managed to take in a show, and by chance bumped into my two old aunts, also travelling to the island. Most of the sea ferry trip to Douglas from Liverpool I spent lying down in a cabin, as there was a very nasty and choppy sea running.

Port St. Mary I knew already, having been there for three lovely weeks the previous year on an engagement vacation, Grandpa's father acting as a chaperone. Grandpa had complained bitterly then, that his father monopolised more of my company than was necessary. During our six week honeymoon I met many of Grandpa's old friends from his schooldays. We went everywhere in a delightful little train which stopped every few minutes at quaint stations full of flowers, particularly fuchsias, whole hedges of them lining the cuttings. Whichever window one looked through, the sea was always in view. In the evenings we'd go to Douglas to see one of their first class shows. Horse drawn trams went along the sea front at Douglas, as they do to this very day, providing a unique experience for many a holidaymaker.

We stayed in an attractive white house, a few yards from the beach, run by a Mrs. Appleby, who did all the cooking. We bought what food we wanted and gave it to her to prepare, a common practice at seaside resorts in those days, long before they become totally disfigured by high rise monstrosities of hotels and apartment blocks. Meals were eaten in our own private dining room. There was no electricity of course, oil lamps being lit in the evenings when it got dark.

With a nine hole golf course practically on our doorstep, Grandpa decided to start teaching me how to play golf. Some clubs were hired and off we went. Grandpa tee'd up a ball, gave me a wooden driver and said, "Right, hit that", standing well away to my right. I hit the ball all right, but it didn't go off in the intended direction. Grandpa let out a scream of pain. I'd got him squarely on the kneecap!! The lesson came to a sudden end, and after the situation had cooled down a bit he said, "How the hell you managed to do that just defeats me." There wasn't any answer to that, was there! In years to come I developed a great love for golf, playing on every possible opportunity. Many rounds were marked by incidents of one sort or another. On the Haslar Course, for example, a hissing and snapping swan rushed at me from behind as I was placing a ball ready to drive off. Intent on mischief it came at me, wings outstretched, from the creek alongside the course. What had provoked the bird I know not, but it was certainly very angry and I had to make a hurried retreat.

Our honeymoon on the Isle of Man is full of wonderful memories, really happy and peaceful times amidst surroundings of such natural beauty that one caught one's breath time and time again. The lap of the seas on the shore and the scream of seagulls are as fresh in my mind now as if I'd heard them only moments ago.

Vast numbers of seagulls screamed and wheeled across the skies around the herring fleet and gutting tables, the chief industry there in those days. Sturdy, hessian aproned Scottish lassies, heads wrapped in shawls, unloaded the barrels of herring from each boat at the long stone pier, their bare, muscular arms glistening with moisture. Next, each girl would set to work gutting the fish at such a speed that the eye could scarce follow their flashing knives. The cleaned fish going to an empty barrel, the entrails would be flung to the ground, to be grabbed by a hurtling white scavenger almost before the scraps landed. A cat accustomed to visiting this scene, crouching behind a bollard hoping to catch a seagull, was itself surprised.

One bird, perhaps having had many near misses, turned the tables, grabbed the cat and took it far out to sea before dropping it to a watery grave. Just retribution I'd call it. Men crying out, "Fresh fish, fresh fish", could be heard early every day as they came round with their barrows to sell mackerel which hadn't left the sea more than ten minutes before.

We met many charming, interesting and delightful people on the Isle of Man. A doctor, his wife, their two children and nanny; the Skillicorns, whom Grandpa had known from his childhood days. Another family with whom we became acquainted were deeply interested in crab fishing. We enjoyed a crab supper with them, although I couldn't watch the crabs being cooked in a copper cauldron when I found out that they were thrown in alive! So many nice people. They all made such a fuss of us that we were very sorry to have to go after six weeks that had simply flown past.

Dear Grandpa. He always suffered from the illusion that by choosing a bride so much younger than himself meant total domination; all he had to do was to "mould" me into the desired pattern!! In this respect, and others, he was a throw back to the Victorian Age. I tried hard to give the impression of being "moulded", and was quite successful at it much of the time but, believe me, I wasn't to be "moulded". Those of you who are still with us will remember his strong character very well and will understand that it was like living with a time bomb. Looking back, many of the situations he placed me in were really hysterically funny, but didn't seem so at the time! Quite often I'd pack a bag and leave him, but always did I return; all would be sweetness and light again — for at least a week! It's often said that opposites attract; this I believe to be true. To be sure our marriage was NEVER boring, I'll say that. I know he was as deeply fond of me as I was of him, but he certainly never made a point of showing it! Recently I've had what for me is irrefutable proof of his care and love since he passed over, and he's even communicated his regret that he made my life so difficult, especially in later years. So he must be very aware of my love and gratitude for his help, of which I am daily very conscious.

But wait, I hear you ask, what about your life before you met Grandpa? Where were you born? What can you tell us about your parents and grandparents? Where did you live? What did you do as a child and teenager?

Good questions. Let me see how well I can recall those far off days, the people, the places and the many events that filled my life.

CHAPTER 2
Childhood Memories

Early years. Our ancestors

My father was born in 1877, and my mother in 1874. They were engaged for five years which in those days meant "walking out very formally and sedately" and not living together in the manner of today. Even so, my father's family were furious, mother being made to feel most unwelcome. One of the many reasons was that my father hadn't brought any of his male friends along to meet his unmarried older sisters, as was customary in those times, with the object of starting up a romance. In this case I dare say it looked pretty hopeless to him, as I well remember him saying that the nearest Aunt Cissy ever got to a man, was when she came out of church and shared an umbrella with one! The whole family disliked mother. She was a pretty, shy girl, with a complexion they declared must have come from using rouge. Mother's complexion needed no rouge or any other artificial addition whatsoever but they never failed to seize any opportunity they could of finding some fault with her. My father announced their engagement, in the middle of the usual formal drawing room tea. Grandfather, deeply religious but always domineering, aggressive and often sadistic, promptly threw a cup of tea at my father, but missed completely, and the drawing room had to be completely repapered.

10

left, Margot: Frieda Marguerite Blundstone
— b. 10th September 1903; d. 1st June 1947
— my only sister.
right, Mother: Maggie Blundstone neé
Walker — b. 13th April 1874; d. 11th August
1952.

All of my earliest recollections are of the then pleasant
Nottinghamshire village of Gedling where my parents went to
live, and the house where I was born in 1908 when my only sister,
Margot, was five. I rather think she resented my arrival, as is not
unusual for an only child of that age who has been the centre of
attention for several years. Hearing church bells ringing always
brings back vivid memories, of times buried deep in my

Father: Cecil Thomas William Blundstone —
b. 15th January 1877; d. June 1921.

subconscious, of fields and daisies, starched Holland pinafores,
alpaca coats and a garden swing that was the chief delight of my
life. I was taken to church at a very early age to sit beside my
parents with my view of everything going on entirely obscured
by the pew in front. I soon discovered that a whispered request
that I needed to spend a penny, always drew immediate results
and, thankfully, I was taken home. The parson's wife tactfully
suggested that if I brought my teddy bear it would help to
distract me from wanting to go home! Nothing did though, and
ultimately I was left in peace at home.

Routine was the key word in our house, and everything was
done to its strictures. Actually I'm a great believer in routine,

especially so in bringing up children, but, regrettably, this idea seems to have been lost over the years. I was never ever bored, even though I spent so much of my time alone, for I found so much enjoyment in exploring the garden. Most adults don't seem to have the slightest idea what a fascinating place a garden is to a child.

I'd upturn stones and be enchanted by the infinite variety of insect life underneath for hours on end. Tight flower buds I would carefully unfold and unwrap their wrinkled petals. I would pick the bark off the silver birch trees (and get scolded for doing so). Anything that looked remotely edible would be tasted, especially the very young shoots of rhubarb. Then there was always the swing. It was one of those sturdy hand made varieties, with a wide wooden seat on thick ropes which shrank after it had been raining so that I'd have difficulty climbing up on to the seat. It was a joy I even find appealing to this day, when I see my great grand-daughter Sophie finding the same delight, standing up, lying on her stomach, or just sitting and swinging.

Part of our ever present routine was the afternoon "walk up the hills"! Mother usually took me, and always the pram came too, even though I begged to walk. Once we came to a very large horse trough full of water at the foot of the hills with a small boy leaning over the side with his little feet well off the ground quite oblivious to our presence. Busy poking a floating match box with a stick trying to make it sink he was murmuring, "Titanic, Titanic!". So it must have been 1912, when I was four. Loving to have a joke with any child, and finding his posterior irresistible she seized him by the seat of his pants saying, "I'll give you Titanic, you rascal, if you fall head first into that you'll think you are on the Titanic!" I well remember that everyone was talking of the terrible disaster at that time. "The hills" as we always called them, eventually flattened out with corn fields besides the lane with its wayside poppies, and entrancing piles of wayside stones, stored there ready for road mending. The traction engine that did the work was a very familiar sight on the roads in those days. I loved to run up and down the mini mountains of stones, much to my mother's annoyance. Quite rightly, she said it ruined the toes and heels of my little red walking shoes. Always, did I plead to walk and not ride in the "sitting up" type of pram known in those days as a "mail cart": a large hefty thing. I was delighted if allowed to get out and push it always with my mother's guiding hand on the handle of course. At one point the lane we always used was bordered by a very deep ditch, filled with enormous nettles. Once, I'd pestered to walk and having been lifted out took the opportunity to grab the mail cart and set off at speed. Swerving out of control both cart and I tumbled into the ditch, the heavy pram coming to rest on top of me, crushing me into the nettles. Mother screamed as well as me, as she was quite unable to climb down into the deep ditch to help me. I don't remember who or how I was rescued, but I do remember only so well how much those nettles stung!

Actually, in those days our clothes were a greater protection than today's would be. We were well covered, even to tiny kid gloves (put on and done up with a button hook every day!). I still have those little brown kid gloves, each with a tiny square missing in the palm, that my mother had cut out saying, "Tiny hands get hot and sticky and this will let the air in!!" Looking at them now, judging by their size, I couldn't have been older than about eighteen months when I first wore them.

Gedling was known as a mining village, for there were so many "collieries" as we called them, around the area. It didn't seem to affect the village in any way though, except that each day, after their shift, the young colliers used to pass our house absolutely soot black from head to toe, but they always appeared to be a happy and cheerful lot. Fully dressed and waiting to go for my walk one day, I was swinging on the garden gate when they passed. One gave me a cheeky smile and said, "Hello baby, waiting for your walk", pulling my bonnet strings tight as he spoke. I fled to mother in great distress and showed her the black thumb marks on the white satin bonnet ribbons tied under my chin!

When my father had his two houses built in Gedling, he was asked, by the Council I presume to name the two roads which met at a right angle where they had been built. Being a great scholar and lover of poetry, he chose the names of Tennyson and Waverley Avenues. Our own house was naturally Waverley, whilst that in Tennyson Avenue was called Fairview. These names remain extant to this day. Close by, at the end of Waverley Avenue, there was a tiny shop which sold sweets. When I was old enough (perhaps five and a half), I was allowed to take my pennies to see what Mr. Sadler had in his gaily coloured collection and maybe buy some "satin cushions", which he'd put into a cone shaped bag. I didn't much care to go out, even this tiny distance, on my own, for any village children I met would pull faces and poke their tongues out at me! My sister, if she was with me, would see them off in no ordinary manner. Five years older than me, with a definite and dominant character, afraid of nothing and no one, on such occasions as these, she was quite invaluable! I was always a bit apprehensive of her, but as she was already at school didn't see her much, as I was still a baby at home.

My hard and arrogant paternal grandfather, was Secretary of the Trent Navigation Company, my father, his only son, being employed in the same concern. Of totally different characters they soon quarrelled, my father walking out on him never to return. To add to my parents distress, my father now let himself be persuaded by a very glib rogue of a Frenchman, to invest all his money in a French typewriting firm. Supposedly a marvellous venture, soon to make him very rich, my poor father quickly discovered the truth after a fruitless visit to Paris. There was no firm and no Frenchman, the rogue having completely disappeared. Total disaster! The Bank reclaimed the two houses my father had built so optimistically at the time of his marriage, and we had to move on, to my mother's intense grief and doubtless to his as well.

I clearly remember those first six, happy years of my life. Margot and I had a French governess. Being so young, not surprisingly I spoke French before English. My mother told me that when the governess left, I spoke a very garbled mixture of both, and no one could understand me! The governess must have loved me, as for years afterwards she always sent me daffodils on my birthday. Sadly, I don't remember her.

We went to Mansfield when I was six and a half. It was September, and World War I had just started. Apart from a few isolated incidents, it didn't seem to make any great impact on my life at that time. The house we went to was nowhere near as nice as the one at Gedling. Mother grieved but made the best of it. Strangely I don't remember noticing the difference. My father became a chartered accountant, setting up in the town on his own. His health, never first class, deteriorated as he worked day and night to recover his resources, and in only seven years he was dead.

I remember my seventh birthday well, and even some of the presents I received — crayons, colouring books etc. Children are more resilient than grown ups I imagine, or at least I was, because I had no difficulty in coping with the troubled times. We had a deep dark cold cellar that came in useful when the zeppelins came over. I found sitting with blankets and a hot drink throughout the night rather stimulating and exciting. This soon gave way to panic though when I heard the zeppelins roar past overhead on their way to bomb Nottingham. Some of the earliest bombs fell on Arkwright Street. I remember being taken to view the damage and listen to the gory tales of casualties, with some people being killed and others injured. Sometimes the sound of tramping feet outside would bring us rushing to the door, and to the nearby Bottle Lane where Canadian troops in training were passing through on a route march. Mostly, they were billeted at Clipstone Camp a few miles from us. It was considered patriotic to invite a few of these chaps into our homes for hot food and hospitality. Mother eagerly fell in with this idea and I remember sitting down at the dining table with cheerful laughing strangers who spoke English but with a strange accent.

Long before this, my love of dancing occupied my every thought and every hope. Thursday afternoon was the highlight of my week when I was taken to Dancing Class clutching my little blue velvet "Dorothy Bag" (and who will remember that name?). Black wool stockings were peeled off revealing dainty white cotton openwork socks, and, oh my!, the ecstasy of slipping on the bronze dancing pumps, crossing the elastic over ones instep, and emerging like a little being from another world! Mothers and Nannies sat around the large "chalked" floor, french chalk having been used to give it an extra polish. Years later mother told me that as she sat watching this room full of hopefuls, her next door neighbour began to chat with her, remarking about me as we filed past, "Now that is what I call a lovely child." Mother was extremely proud, saying, "That one's mine."

So life moved on as did the horror of World War I. My mother often sat holding the newspaper on her knee with tears pouring down her face as she read the daily casualty lists. The slaughter, beyond all description, didn't come to an end until I was eleven, in 1918, when I heard at school having been summoned into the main hall with everyone else, to hear that the Armistice had been signed.

I went to my first school, a kindergarten about half a mile from our house, when I was about six and a half. This was run by a Miss Durand, of French extraction I think, sometimes assisted by Miss Ruth Burney, although she chiefly taught us dancing. It was mornings only for both little boys and girls, all about my own age. I loved it! Held in the Methodist Church Hall, close by the Methodist Church, there was a large grassy area between the buildings where we would spend our mid-morning break. Here we'd open our little lunch boxes, and eat the Bovril sandwiches, apples or whatever else our mothers had prepared for us. To this day, the smell of Bovril takes me straight back to the age of six in the playground. One or two of those children remained my friends even after I became an adult. Doreen Burgin, for example, two years older than me, and one of the three girls who drove in the little Austin 7 from Mansfield to Nottingham to be at my wedding. Eventually Doreen became Jocelyn's Godmother, and when she got married spent part of her rather unusual honeymoon camping on our lawn at Weymouth. Asked why she'd chosen such a spartan start to her married life, she told me that Eric's doctor advised it on health grounds. It transpired he had tuberculosis and later they spent some time in Switzerland. Lovely, blonde and athletic Doreen had to wait to have any children but did so eventually before getting T.B. herself, dying before she was even thirty.

I also met Rupert at my kindergarten, my greatest childhood friend. A year younger than me, he was an artistic, adventurous boy. He loved me to read to him, although as his mother said quite correctly, he was only lazy and could read well himself. Nevertheless I was for ever willing to read to him from the piles of books he brought back from the library, books like "Tanglewood Tales" and "Beyond the Blue Mountains", I recall. We spent much time together, exploring the lanes and byways and getting chased off by irate farmers. When his mother asked us what we would do when we grew up, we were quite certain, replying in chorus, "We are going to live together and form a circus!!" Once he said to me, "Carlene, there's no-one at home, let's go there and make something special". The something special turned out to be a melted bar of chocolate with sugar stirred in together with the entire cream of the top of the milk. Milk didn't come in bottles of course, but was carried to the door in an urn, to be ladled out into a "pancheon", a sort of basin, to be left on a marble slab in the pantry to keep cool. The cream would rise to the surface and could then be scooped off with a spoon. I feel sure that Rupert's mother often wondered where the cream had gone, and had she guessed he'd have been in dead trouble. A beautiful woman, an extremely firm mother, even a bit narsh sometimes, I thought, but part of a most handsome family, though I didn't notice it until I was a good deal older. Rupert and I drifted apart over the next few years. Eventually I came across him again at swimming gala I'd gone to with Margot. We spotted an Adonis like figure poised at the edge of the bath with the other competitors, and my sister said, "Good heavens, surely that's Rupert White". And so it was, and when he emerged from the pool, he called out my name, and rushed round to talk to me, shaking the water from his thick black hair. I was overjoyed to see him, his face unchanged, still with those deep blue almond shaped eyes and long black eyelashes. He called to see us twice after that meeting. The second time he told me "Carlene, you've got the most beautiful eyebrows I've ever seen". I was so taken aback I've no idea how I replied. A great wave of sadness swept over me as I realised that this imp with a succession of scabs on his knees, gained from falling out of scores of trees could now be only a memory. I knew I could never think of him in any other way than as the dearest companion I'd ever had, someone who'd shared all my childhood, and now I'd lost him for good. After this encounter I confess I dodged seeing him as much as possible, though it grieved me to do so. I still think very tenderly of those far off days.

Until I was sixteen, my dear mother cherished an ambition that I'd make music my career! She spent eight years of hope and money she could ill afford, on my music lessons. I always knew it was hopeless for even though I passed my exams, I never imagined I'd attain the heights she hoped for. Sight reading was my downfall really, although I could memorise anything in a very short time. I can recall with complete clarity the day my music lessons finally came to end. It was my sixteenth birthday and I turned up for my lessons as usual but must have somehow referred to the fact that it was my birthday. On hearing this news, my music master grabbed me fiercely and showered me with very passionate kisses, saying things like "Sweet sixteen and never been kissed before," etc. While I struggled and fought off his ginger moustache I thought, "This is it, this is the end of my music lessons." It was. When I told my mother about it, enraged, she wrote him a letter immediately terminating my lessons. About ten years ago, I fell in love with my piano and it's become one of my most treasured possessions that I just couldn't live without. I still can't sight read to any degree, of course, but get hours of delight playing Irving Berlin (who couldn't sight read either), Noel Coward, Gershwin and others. So, although mother's hopes and ambitions for me didn't turn out as she wanted, her efforts have brought me hours and hours of deep relaxing happiness, when I can escape into a past and forget the problems of today.

Memories of my paternal Grandparents, the Blundstones, who lived at Mapperley on the outskirts of Nottingham, never fade. I wish I could say they were pleasant ones. Gedling being close by, my parents would take me in the mail cart to have tea with them on Sunday afternoons. Mother didn't enjoy these trips but went for my father's sake, who went himself as a dutiful son. I have clear, horrible recollections of the tricks my sadistic Grandfather would get up to. Dressed and sitting in my mail cart,

left, My Paternal Grandfather: William Henry Blundstone — b. 13th April 1845. *right, My Paternal Grandmother:* Keturah Ann Blundstone — b. 21st June 1845; m. 3rd July 1869.

"Carisbrook" — The Mapperly house where they lived and of very mixed memories.

quite unsuspecting and innocently waiting for my parents to take me home, my sadistic grandfather would creep up silently behind me, take the pram handles and swiftly dip them right down to the ground, just to hear me scream in fright. My mother was furious but he never stopped doing it from time to time. Years later, when I was about twelve, I had to spend a duty week with them, (how I disliked such visits), and endure more of his sadistic "jokes", like filling my sponge bag with nettles, so that when I reached into it for anything, I'd get soundly stung. He found this very amusing, chuckling like a fiend. Grandmother was a tiny pale completely dominated little creature, meek, mean and cold. She always greeted me with the words, "Have you got a kiss for me?", and present me with a reluctant cheek that I had to stand on tip toe to reach. My mother, all her life, only mentioned them with intense distaste, telling me how when my sister Margot was born twelve months after her marriage, they declared it "in quite disgusting haste". When baby Margot was proudly presented to grandmother for admiration, all she did was sniff. My mother exclaimed, enthusiastically, "Isn't she lovely", only to get the cold response, "Well, I suppose every mother thinks that."

Grandmother Blundstone died in 1921 when I was thirteen, just five months before my father. There had been a prolonged rift between us before and I hadn't seen them for quite a while. The two Aunts paid us occasional visits, which Margot and I tried to avoid, at least in part, by being out when they arrived. They descended on us when grandmother died demanding, in the manner of it was my duty, that I go back to Mapperley with them to stay until after the funeral. Mother would have said no, but, overshadowed by their presence, reluctantly agreed. I wish she hadn't for I'll never forget that episode. It was January, and got dark early, so, by the time we reached "Carisbrook" the Mapperley house, gas lamps had already been lit. My thirteen year old mind was filled with horror for I knew that somewhere within its wall lay a dead body. I was shown my bedroom and told to be down to supper in ten minutes. Every closed door took on a sinister meaning for me. In those days, when anyone died, they were always kept in the house, indeed, I don't think there were any funeral parlours as there are today. I had supper but still didn't know where my grandmother lay. Then, to my utter horror, Aunt Ann said, "Would you like to see Grandma now?" I longed to scream "No!, No!, No!", but such was their influence, I meekly agreed. She was laying in an open coffin in the centre of the drawing room. The gas lights burning dimly beside the fireplace enhanced the eerie and macabre atmosphere. Gently, I was led to the side of the coffin. To this very day, every feature of that wax life effigy is imprinted on my mind. She looked exactly like a witch, her sunken mouth, as is usual for those who have had false teeth, making her already prominent nose even more "witch like". Totally horrified, I slowly edged away, but Aunt Ann, still grasping my arm then said, "Would you like to kiss her?" From somewhere I found the courage to murmur, "No thank you". I don't really remember the funeral, for I couldn't chase this shocking experience from my mind. I only remember the smell of hyacinths, as these pretty flowers predominated in the piles of wreaths stacked in the hall. I'm glad, though, that my haunting memories never put me off their lovely perfume.

Having described my father's parents, in what seems to me appropriately unlovely terms, I must stress how totally different my dear gentle loving father was himself. But, by now you will probably be saying, "What about your mother though? What about her life? You've told us nothing about her yet". Well, she was a completely different character to me. Quiet dignified and rather aloof, making many people think she was snobbish, which was far from the truth. She did have a very dark secret though, so dark in fact that I didn't hear of it until I was quite grown up. It was most skillfully concealed and whether or not her brothers and sisters knew of it, I've no idea. I must tell you of this "skeleton in our closet".

Mother's grandparents were very prosperous farmers and country landowners going by the name of Clark, so I was told. From the snatches of information I managed to get from my mother, their daughter, Maria, my grandmother, decided life at home on the farm wasn't quite what she wanted. It seems she was a perfectly normal and lively little thing, with an addiction for reading love stories, and a passion for the theatre. She told her mother that her idea of bliss would be to live next door to the Theatre! So, realising Maria would need a bit more in her life than farming, and being extremely fond of children herself, my grandmother secured Maria a situation in a gentleman's household to train as a nursery nurse. In those mid-Victorian days it was not particularly unusual for a member of the male gentry with a large staff, to think it was his perogative to seduce any one he fancied. This gentleman fancied my grandmother, made her pregnant, and in due course my mother was born. It was bad enough in those days for a girl to be pregnant without a wedding ring, but in this case the scandal was very much worse. Her horrified parents rallied round her, "closing ranks" so to

Ann Hodgson Grandmother Born 1773.
William Hodgson Grandfather Born Ap 3rd 1763.
Daughta
Sarah Hodgson Daughter Born Sept 22nd 1805.
Keturah Hodgson   "   "   Aug. 12th 1807.
Thomas Hodgson Son   "   Aug. 4th 1809.
William Hodgson   "   "   June 23rd 1812.
Robert Hodgson   "   "   April 28th 1815.

Thomas Hodgson Father born Aug 9th 1809.
Ann Hodgson née Steward Mother   "   March 4th 1810 or 1811.
                                          Died Dec 31st 1869.
          Married August 31 1842 Sneinton Church
Sarah-ann Hodgson Born Dec 12th St Pierre Calais 1843.
Keturah-Ann Hodgson Born June 21st   " 1845.
William Louis Hodgson Born Sept 14th Sneinton Nott 1847.
Thomas Uriah Hodgson   "   Nov 18th Nott 1849.
Mary Ann Hodgson   "   Sept 15th Nott 1852.
Alfred Swales Hodgson   "   Jan 28th Nott 1855.
          Joseph Osborn Hodgson son of above
          died 30th Dec 1898

William Henry Blundstone (Father) Born April 13th 1843.
Keturah Ann Blundstone   (mother) June 21st 1847
          Married July 3rd 1869 at Holy Trinity Ch Nott
Ann Blundstone daughter Born May 15th 1870.
Elizabeth Blundstone daughter Born May 15th 1870.
                    Died May 19th 1870.
Elizabeth Keturah Blundstone Born April 30th 1872
                    died 5 Jan 1939

speak, very swiftly getting her married to a most willing admirer
(by whom she later had ten more children). In 1910, aged fifty
three she was thrown out of a trap she was driving when the
horse reared unexpectedly, receiving injuries from which she
later died. I was two at the time, so I only vaguely remember what
she looked like.

What made my mother confide her dark secret to me in the
middle of her life I've no idea, except that perhaps she may have

Cecil Thomas William Blundstone von Born 15 Jan 1877
Died June 1921

Cecil Thomas William Blundstone Father Jan 15 1877
Married & thomas Died June 19th -21
Maggie Walker (mother) born 13 April 1874

Daughter
Frieda Marguerite Blundstone born Sept 12 1903

Daughter
Daisy Carlene Blundstone born March 22 1908

Arnold Ashworth Pomfret Born Blackpool 1st June 1900 (Father)
married (mother)
Daisy Carlene Blundstone Born Gedling 22 Nov 1908

1st Daughter
Jill Blundstone Pomfret Born Alverstoke 21 Sep 1929

2nd Daughter
Jocelyn Leslie Blundstone Born 1st June 1932
Simonstown Sth Africa
John Stephen Pomfret Born Dec 2nd 1950
at Southsea. Hants

Some of Our Ancestors. The hand written listing on these two pages is a copy made by my Aunt Ann (Blundstone) from an original record in a historic family Bible which I expected to come into my possession. Regrettably this did not come about, so I'm very glad my Aunt let me have this handwritten copy of the important records noted on its flyleaf.

felt it was her duty to do so. I've no idea when she found out herself. Extremely reticent on the subject she wouldn't talk about it at all beyond the mere facts, and even these had to be coaxed out of her very tactfully. I asked her once if she ever found out who her real father was. "Yes," she replied quite calmly. "Did you ever go to see him?", I gently prodded. "Once," she said, "As a child, I was taken to see him." She didn't of course, know then who he was. He had been pleasant and kind, and cupped her

Births and Christening Records. Records in my
mother's own handwriting of births and christenings
in my branch of the family. Jill's birth is included,
but not that of Jocelyn so this record was made soon
after 1929. Not only are the dates of birth noted but
also the exact times!

little face in his hands and gazed at her very thoughtfully. That's
all I managed to get out of her. And that wasn't easy. Perhaps its
no surprise that she never had anything in common with the rest
of her large family and drifted away from them. Her "official"
father, I remember well. Many years after my Grandmother
Maria died, he visited us occasionally, coming in his very smart

pony trap. We used to love to listen with excitement, to Dolly's hoofs clip clopping along the lane, and give her sugar lumps. To me he looked exactly like a replica of a genial Santa Claus, with his snow white beard, but somewhere I heard that he was often far from kind to my little grandmother. So my real grandfather is wrapped in mystery and will remain that way, I'm afraid.

It amuses me a lot to think of the impact this "dark secret" would have had on my formal and ice cold Blundstone grandparents. Had they known of it — or even suspected it might exist — to say they would have liked my mother even less is a gross understatement!

Grandpa Walker was the figure we knew, though we didn't see much of him. He died at sixty three, having married again, and lost his second wife from cancer, after she had bourne him one child who was left an orphan at the age of six. Fortunately his wealthy New Zealand sheep farming relatives came over to get him; hopefully the poor lad found comfort and happiness in a very different life. I wonder if my mother would approve of me telling you her "dark secret". I certainly feel a sense of guilt at having done so, but anyway, she had no reason to feel any shame for something she'd had nothing to do with herself? No more have I! Everybody involved has long been in the next world now, and their standards will have changed completely about anything to do with this world. I'm sure that by now my mother is aware of how little her "dark secret" really matters. I've always found it a very intriguing and fascinating story with positively nothing about it to make me feel any "shame". How many families, if one dug deep enough, would not have something similar to reveal. Not many I guess. I trust that you will find it as interesting as I to find out a little about the kind of roots we have sprung from, and what their lives were like. Very similar situations are happening every day now, the only difference being that nobody tries to conceal them any more, and, if the people are important enough, they make the headlines. My recollections may make my children and their children wonder how it can be that we are all descended from such ice cold individuals, when we are all so exuberant, demonstrative and loving to each other. Perhaps they didn't have hearts and emotions like us. I don't know. Wherever they are now, I hope they will forgive me, for truthfully recording the incidents which stand out in my memory. I hope so. It's incredible to think that when all these events occurred, they were much younger than I am now, for, of course, I'm the longest living member of this family, still not departed yet!

CHAPTER 3
My Teenage Twenties

Dancing, tennis, parties — happy times

During my teenage years I never knew hardship although I am sure my mother did. Somehow we got through though. Girls wouldn't dream of taking a job in those days, unless one was specially trained for it, so Margot and I were no asset, as all we wanted to do was dance. This meant ballet and a dancing school of course, which was such an important part of my exciting teenage years in the nineteen twenties.

When I began this story, one of my pert grand-daughters said, "You'll put in all the spicy bits won't you grandma?" "Knowing you", I replied, "and your interpretation of 'spicy bits', the answer is definitely NO". Wails of protest followed my rejoinder of course, but it occurs to me that some details of my life before I came across Grandpa might make interesting and entertaining reading. By today's standards, young people might think the "gay twenties" rather tame: they don't know what they missed though. For example, I had my first proposal of marriage at sixteen. To say that it came as an extreme shock is putting it mildly. It came about from my great friendship with the Bramelds.

Mr. and Mrs. Brameld were the dearest friends I've ever had, they almost regarded me as the daughter they never had themselves. I got on well with their only child Dick, two years older than me, in a wonderful sort of semi platonic way really, although he'd chase me around and sometimes I had to resist a snatched kiss. But there was never anything sentimental, his practical jokes driving me round the bend. Mr. Brameld was manager of the Westminster Bank in The Square at Retford. He was a darling, a tall, gentle, quiet soul devoted to his little vivacious wife. I'm sure they were as fond of me as I was of them. They asked me over to their house many, many times, to hunt balls, tennis club dances and tournaments and so on. I spent weeks on end there motoring around in their Harper Bean car, a make unheard of today, doing all the cinemas and shows. Both were most enthusiastic golfers and that's how I came to get my proposal of marriage. The young man involved was by way of being a bit of a golf celebrity, having a handicap of plus 4, and was staying with them in a small house party. One afternoon Mrs. Brameld gave me a basket, told me where to find a long ladder, and sent me to pick cherries from a tall tree. I'd climbed up, and was busy picking at the top of this tall ladder, when up sauntered this young man, much older than me and chatted with me for a few minutes. I quite forget his name, that's how interested I was in him! Then, out of the blue, he went on, "Have you ever thought about marriage?" Taken aback, all I could think of to say was, "Goodness no, I'm only sixteen you know!" There was a pause, and then he said, "Would you consider marriage with me?" Extreme shock is the only way to describe my feelings, as I turned and looked down at his upturned face and was aghast to see that he was deadly serious. I was so embarrassed I can't really remember how I replied, but I know I responded very firmly; I wasn't thinking of marrying at all, and certainly not at my age. He said he'd wait! (I thought the poor chap would have a long wait!) As kindly as I could I thanked him for his offer, but the answer was still no! Subsequently I avoided him. I never told anyone, not even the Bramelds or my other young friends. It gave me something to ponder on though! If Dick had found out he'd have teased the very life out of me!

Dick was an absolutely marvellous dancer. We loved dancing with each other for the sheer coordination and rhythm of smoothly knowing exactly what one's partner was going to do, an infinite joy that only good dancers can experience. In those days people were taught how to dance, to listen to rhythm. Nowadays I find it quite hilarious to watch what passes for "dancing"; couples walk onto the dance floor, then begin ridiculous jerks and twists and flapping of arms, with their so called partner all of six feet away. My scrap book contains most of my dance programmes from the mid twenties with their little pencils attached. Given out at the beginning of the ball, there was a breathtaking time watching who came up to ask one for a dance and to have their name written in for the foxtrot, waltz or quickstep. It was an anxious time if one didn't see ones "interest of the moment" coming, perhaps he'd been held up on the other side of the ballroom? After all, once the programme was filled that was it! One couldn't ask anyone to cancel a dance in favour of someone else, that would never do! Unless it was dear Mr. Brameld of course, who would say, "If there's someone else you'd like don't hesistate to cross my name out." (But I'd always ask him first.) At dances we were always accompanied by the grown-ups. We shouldn't have enjoyed it otherwise. They were part of the scene; knowing they were there gave me a wonderful warm feeling of confidence, even though I saw little of them during the evening, as they would stay with their own friends. The first time I tasted champagne was at the Grove Hunt Ball at the usual magnificent midnight spread. For this occasion I'd put up my hair into "Chelsea Buns", to make myself look older, as I was under the age limit and not supposed to be there at all!

Any ball or dance that finished before 3 a.m. we considered a dead loss. After the dance we would all go back to Bank House for more fun and games and more eats, 'til Mrs. Brameld decided it was time we all went to bed. Several of the boys worked in the Bank and had to be up early next day. I adored Mrs. Brameld, she was tiny, neat, with large china blue eyes, and neat white shingled hair. Always game for anything, she had, nevertheless, a compelling voice of authority when it was needed, as it sometimes was with Dick. At 18 his practical jokes went right over the top at times, hysterically funny we all thought, but I for one didn't let him know it. To this very day I shudder with horror when I think of some of his many escapades. One I recall particularly vividly.

Margery, Dick's cousin and a school friend of mine, was staying with us and sharing my bedroom. One night, very late, we were lying in bed, chattering about all those things that sixteen year olds love to talk about, when a creak seemed to come from the wardrobe door. Stopping dead, "What was that?" we said. Presently, another creak, unmistakable this time. We held our breath and gazed in horror at the wardrobe as a hand appeared around the door. The eerie sight in the shaft of midsummer moonlight almost stopped our hearts beating. Time seemed to stand still and then the tension shattered as a figure sprang out with a whoop. It was Dick! Not content with this performance he then climbed out of our window overlooking the Square, as did the entire front of Bank House. Petrified, we watched him get onto the minute ledge outside and inch his way towards his own bedroom window, which he'd left open, with a forty foot sheer drop into the Square below him. Even now it turns my stomach over to think of it. We never told his mother of course. More harmless pranks he had an abundance of. Some virtually invisible black cotton would be tied to the hem of my pillow, led out under the door, and when he thought I was half asleep, gently pulled and I'd find my pillow sliding away from under my head. Always there was something. Pepper on the pillow and hard bake breadcrumbs under the bottom sheet were more of his tricks. The contemporary feather beds made it easy to disguise a few lumps; it really hurt when one leapt onto an apparently soft bed to land on some hard object concealed within the sheets. One day I felt I'd have some revenge. Getting a tin of Golden Syrup from the kitchen, I very liberally spread the inside of his carefully folded pyjama trousers with the contents. I listened hard to hear his reaction, but all was quiet except for an unusual number of trips to the bathroom! Next day he passed it off blandly remarking that he'd slept well, no problems. Sometimes his parents heard the noise of these antics, however quiet we tried to be. Once their bedroom door flew open and Mrs. Brameld stood there, catching Dick red-handed with a pillow in his arms, obviously intent on mischief. Fiercely she told him, "I've had enough", adding in tones of great authority, "Get back. Get back to your room at once!". He knew she meant what she said but, as always, tried to make a joke of it shuffling backwards into his room. With a great leap he threw himself onto his bed and as he landed went clean through the springs! It was hilarious to see his expression with his bottom almost touching the floor! With grim satisfaction, Mrs. Brameld slammed his door on this comical scene saying, "And NOW you can sleep on it!"

I treasure my teenage years with the Bramelds so deeply that tears come to my eyes as I look through those old dance programmes, with the pencilled in names of all my different partners and the tunes we danced to played by the superb Conri Tates band.

Now and then all of us had a "crush" on some particular chap or another; often they didn't even know! I well remember one boy, Ralph Burton, I found quite attractive. Once at a Hunt

Ball he actually led me behind a potted fern and kissed me! A most enterprising young man, he came to Mansfield where I lived and not knowing my surname was Blundstone, of all difficult names, nothing daunted, circled around in his scarlet sports car, calling at various houses. At each he asked if they knew of a widow with a daughter called Carlene!! Eventually he found me. Many an innocent jaunt I enjoyed in that open sports car, calling in to farms to have tea. I was introduced to another nice young man by a great friend, Mary Merryweather who was a fellow student at the Gilmer School of Dancing. Her cousin, John Merryweather was a sweet boy who went up in my estimation by cycling many miles from Southwell to see me, bringing two dozen gorgeous red roses in his saddlebag! I think I must have had the pick of the Merryweather nurseries which his family owned.

By now I was sixteen and a working student, training to be a dancer at the Gilmer School in Nottingham, where my sister Margot was by now a qualified teacher. I grew to love the other girls of my own age I met there, many becoming life long friends. Our life was rigid, hard working but more than interesting. The proprietor was a Miss Schofield, known to us as "Schoie". Firm, kind, and generous she became a lifelong friend, as did the housekeeper secretary, "Mummy" Fowkes. Both were in their forties, appearing terribly mature to us. Quite rightly they regulated our lives to an extent present day girls would rebel against. Nine thirty was the dead line when we went out for an evening, and we had to say where we were going and who with. Even a few minutes late in and they'd be waiting with a very stern lecture and the announcement that we were too late for supper! One night I persuaded a maid to save me some supper, sneaking in late. I was in the basement kitchen when, suddenly, I heard Schoie's footsteps trotting down the stairs on her way, no doubt, to water her hyacinth bulbs. I heard her calling out to Doris, "Miss Blundstone isn't in yet!". I was, for Doris had just handed me a nice plate of supper. Quickly, Doris opened the coal cellar door, pushed me in and slammed it again. In total darkness, I fell down three steps I'd no idea were there, my plate of supper and I landing uncomfortably amongst a heap of coals. Schoie stayed talking to Doris for so long I felt I'd never see daylight again.

Schoie, then about 48 and a spinster, suddenly astonished us all by getting married to a Mr. Frisby, "Frizzy" to us, a dear man that we girls liked. Looking back I rather fancy he liked us too. He was twelve years younger than Schoie, an age gap I think

Programme.	Engagements.
Programme.	**Engagements.**

C. Blumstone

Programme.		Engagements.
1 Valse ... Underneath the Mellow Moon	1	
2 Fox Trot .... Felix kept on Walking	2	
3 Parade Two Step ....On the Road to Anywhere	3	
4 Fox Trot............................Every Day	4	
5 Fox Trot............................Moon Love	5	
6 Lancers .... Russian	6	
7 Fox Trot ....My Sweetie went away	7	
8 One Step .... Oom-pah	8	
9 Valse .... Down the Ohio	9	
10 Fox Trot. Last night on the Back Porch	10	
11 Schottische.................Fragrant Roses	11	
12 Fox Trot ...... Dirty Hands, Dirty Face	12	
13 Valse .... Honey, dat's all	13	
14 One Step .... Some One	14	
15 Fox Trot.................Maggie! Yes, Ma	15	
16 Veleta ....Hawaiian Rainbow	16	
17 Fox Trot ....You were meant for me	17	
18 Lancers .... Arcadians	18	
19 Fox Trot .... I love me	19	
20 Valse and John Peel...........Roll along Missouri	20	

Supper after the 9th Dance. when the following Extras will be played:

	EXTRAS:
1 Fox Trot.....................Barney Google	1
2 One Step.............................Joe is here	2
3 Fox Trot ......When the Sun goes down	3

ROWLAND'S   BAND.

One of my dance programmes that I've kept for over 60 years. This one is of the Grove Hunt Staff Ball of Feb 20th 1924. My partners included both Dick and Mr. Brameld (see p.17).

is a recipe for disaster if things prove stormy. However, in this case I believe it all worked moderately well for they were still together when she died thirty years or so later. After marrying she didn't teach quite as much, but continued to appear in most of the classes, being the first to teach us the Charleston. We learnt every type of dancing, and also went to the Nottingham School of Art twice weekly as well as having elocution lessons. One of our teachers was Miss Nesbitt, once a dancer in Pavlova's company. A forceful character of 35, with boundless energy, she bulldozed around the place at great speed. With jutting jaw and resonant voice, we just had to take notice of her. She was alright if one kept in her good books, but she could be very cutting, though, at times.

I've tried not to be at all boring in recounting my recollections of the "twenties" as I know how easily I get carried away remembering those exciting days. I am so very glad I was young then. At the time "Oxford Bags" the men all wore brought many a laugh for the older generation, but to my mind they were preferable to the torn and patched jeans one sees about everywhere now, which aren't even funny. A "relationship", too, an overworked expression which only seems to mean one thing now, seldom went beyond the realms of flirtation. Come to think of it, I don't even seem to hear the word "flirt" any more. In my "salad days" noses were always turned up at a "fast" girl who had too many dates. Not so now, when just about anything seems to be acceptable.

The nineteen twenties have the reputation of being a very liberated era, as of course they were, after the strict constraints of Edwardian and Victorian times. Mercifully no one had the slightest idea to what depths the nineteen eighties would sink, some sixty years later. Without attempting to moralise, it strikes me as sad that some of the joys and the recreations that used to be such fun have been replaced by sinister and unlovely drug taking, porn videos and strip shows not even dreamt of when I was a young girl. All of the fascinating activities I enjoyed so much in the mid-twenties came to an end, when my life suddenly took a new turn. I met someone most of my family came to know as "Grandpa", Pomfret, or "Daddy" as I was most often heard to call him. I've already described at the beginning of this book how our meeting, engagement, marriage and honeymoon took place in just a few years, to change my life for ever. The lovely people I had known, danced with, talked to and whose company I greatly enjoyed during the times I've been describing have mostly long since gone on ahead of me. My belief that I shall meet them again hereafter is very strong. I look forward enormously to my reunion with them all.

CHAPTER 4

Motherhood

*Scarlet fever, mastitis, and an overly
zealous person*

Having interrupted my story to tell you something of my
formative years, of my ancestors and childhood friends, I must
now take up the tale from the point where I left it at the end of
Chapter 1.

After a first class honeymoon on the Isle of Man with my
new husband, the time had now come to begin our married life
in earnest. This started in Gosport. Somebody had
recommended a pub there called The Crown Hotel in the middle
of the town. We booked in for a few days whilst we looked
around for a house. The Crown we found much too delightful
though, being so well looked after that we stayed there for a year
and a half, the owners treating us very well. The Crown is the
oldest hotel in Gosport, really an old pub with a cobblestone yard
outside where horses and drays once carried in loads of beer
barrels. The very few bedrooms were mostly used by commercial
travellers ("reps." these days) who only stayed overnight, so our
quarters were very private. No matter how full the place was I
always got first attention, being attended to by a sweet, rosy
cheeked, plump country girl called Betty who brought meals up

to my room and laid the fires etc. The landlady, Mrs. Dennis, regarded me as "special" I think, as they hadn't had any children of their own. They had adopted a baby girl many years earlier who was then in her twenties. She was a school teacher who I only met twice, but I remember lending her my wedding veil though when she got married.

Soon I became pregnant and Mrs. Dennis literally took charge, mothering me to such an extent that she always referred to my expected child as if it were her own, calling it "my baby". In fact I think she would willingly have given birth to it herself if she could (and believe me she'd have been welcome to that task). When my baby, Jill, was twenty, married and expecting Roger, we were unfortunately out in Bermuda. Close friends of long standing, Jean Robertson and her husband, insisted on having Jill, whose own husband was away at sea, to stay until she went into the nursing home. (And Jill's peke too, of course!) Jill often took her peke, Sheng Tai, on the common for a walk and struck up a casual acquaintanceship with another dog owner. This lady, noticing Jill's condition, brought up the topic of where she lived, where was the baby to be born, was her husband in the Navy and so on. Southsea and Portsmouth were thick with Navy wives in those days so it was a natural enough question. At last she enquired, "Did you ever come across anyone in the Navy called Pomfret?" Jill of course said, "Yes, I'm a Pomfret myself, Jill Pomfret before my marriage". Mrs. Dennis, for that is who Jill had met, was quite astonished to find she was talking to "her baby". Jill naturally didn't know much about Mrs. Dennis's involvement in her birth of course, only knowing that her birthplace had been a nursing home in Anglesey Road, Alverstoke, a residential part of Gosport.

As a young Surgeon Lieutenant attached to the HMS Vincent, the Shore Establishment in Forton Road, Grandpa's duty hours were one day on and one day off. I spent a lot of time alone feeling very sick and ill, lying on the bed feeling quite miserable. Mrs. Dennis came in daily to try and cheer me up, make me eat, and forced me to drink champagne or soup and eat a little to boost me up. She stood by me as I dressed and took me out in her car. Frankly, I don't know how I would have managed without her. My day came eventually and it was she who took me to the nursing home. After a twenty four hour struggle baby arrived at midnight, apparently dead! For over an hour the matron and doctor struggled to revive her. As I was still under the anaesthetic I was only vaguely aware of what was going on. Oxygen tubes were up the baby's nose, brandy was injected into her arm, she was plunged first into hot and then cold water — the doctor even breathed into her mouth. Finally I more or less came round to see the doctor and matron kneeling on the hearth looking despairingly at each other. "Oh my God!", I thought, "This is it, she's dead!" She wasn't though, for gradually a spasmodic cry issued forth from the tiny body. When I finally came round completely, matron queried, "Would you like to see your baby?" "No", I replied, "Not if she's not going to live". They assured me she would so I held that poor little bright red and wrinkled scrap in my arms. All I could bring myself to say was, "Oh, you poor little thing, your poor little thing", over and over again. But from then on she was absolutely no trouble at all — just about the healthiest baby anyone could wish to see. Grandpa was, of course, delighted with his little daughter, sitting on the edge of my bed each day and talking to her as if she could understand everything he was saying.

When Jill was about ten days old, Grandpa decided he'd better arrange a christening, announcing that he'd asked the Rev. Basil Daniels to do this job, also asking him to be her Godfather. The latter idea I found mildly surprising, as he wasn't a close friend really. A dreary, doleful looking character, much older than us, fortyish I'd say. I don't think he liked me very much for I caught his very disapproving eye on my red nail varnish more than once. However, since he was a naval padre at HMS St. Vincent I expect he seemed a suitable choice to Grandpa. Taking me by surprise the worthy cleric decided to pay me an impromptu visit one day at the nursing home when Jill was about ten days old. Having greeted me politely, a chair was pulled up and he sat by my bed, making the usual stilted, desultory conversation. What he didn't know was that I was sitting on a bed-pan! Minutes before he'd arrived a nurse had breezed in with the enjoinder, "Perhaps you'd better sit on this before you have your afternoon nap!" I felt trapped as I didn't have the courage to ask him to fetch a nurse, or to let him know of my predicament. I just sat very still edging the bedclothes around me as discreetly as I could hoping he wouldn't stay long. Oh, but he did, didn't he. Eventually to my great relief he got up as if to go, but no, only to go over and inspect the baby! Then he turned and asked if he could say some prayers!! Now, a bed pan is not a very comfortable thing to sit on at the best of times, but by now it felt as if it had welded itself inseparably to my anatomy, never to be parted from me again. Unknowingly, the well-meaning Rev. knelt down at the foot of Jill's bed and proceeded to pray loudly for some time! So did I, silently, that he'd hurry up and go. I hasten to add I've nothing against his actions in principle. I'm greatly in favour of prayer, at the right time and place. This wasn't either, in my opinion. My prayers were directed at hoping the nurse wouldn't come in and offer him a cup of tea, and then try to recover the bed-pan, for the very last thing I wanted was for him to find out I'd been sat on it throughout his visit. Luckily, she didn't. When, later, they found out that through a misunderstanding I'd been left in this embarassing state, everyone collapsed in mirth. It wasn't so funny at the time though.

One day Grandpa didn't come to see me. Instead my doctor told me that he was very ill indeed in Haslar Hospital with scarlet fever, acquired from examining infected boys at St. Vincent, so ill in fact that it was touch and go whether he lived or not. Much unhappiness was evinced, as the Nursing Home was full of general as well as maternity patients. Everything he'd touched was taken away at once. I now discovered that all was not right with me either as I developed a very large breast abcess. No antibiotics then, of course so I just had to grin and bear it — a hot compress applied now and again giving some relief. It became a real drama though when I developed a most fearful scarlet rash, the doctor diagnosing scarlet fever, no matter how much I argued with him that I'd already had it eighteen months before! He wouldn't have it though. It was too obvious, a husband in one hospital with scarlet fever and now me, sitting there covered in a typical scarlet rash. An ambulance (more like an old baker's van in those days) was obtained at once, baby and I being removed to the fever hospital forthwith. My time there was just too awful an experience to do justice to on paper! Installed in an observation side ward, baby beside me in a cot, in the Diptheria Block, I discovered I was only divided from the diptheria patients by a glass door. Mostly children, they were consumed with curiosity over the baby next door constantly pressing their little noses up against the glass to try and see in. I had to use the same bathroom and wash basin as these children, often at the same time as they were in the room themselves. I heard a nurse tell them, "No, you can't go in there, but I'll bring the baby in here and let you see it one day". I was horrified but, believe it or not, she did just that. I came out of the bathroom one day to see her in the diptheria ward with Jill in her arms saying, "Now stand back a little, please, not TOO near please"! I felt near collapse. To make matters worse, I was now suffering acute pains in my left breast which had swollen alarmingly, baby no longer being able to feed from that side.

Through a mist of pain and misery I still found amusement in one particular incident. Awaking at 5.30 a.m. I found a huge burly porter pushing my bed about. I begged him not to disturb the baby, but too late — she was already being trundled about too and of course woke up demanding food in no uncertain voice. Next a ward maid appearing to make up the open fire. She looked a bit simple but gave me a broad grin and a cheerful "good morning". Conversationally she remarked, "Do you know, a woman died in your bed the day before yesterday". I took this in responding "Oh yes", and, as casually as I could manage, "What did she die of?" "Spotted fever" (highly contagious spinal meningitis), came the prompt reply, adding, "But it's been well disinfected since". So, I thought, if we managed to avoid scarlet fever and diptheria we could still perish from meningitis! A nurse hearing this exchange took her outside and gave her a good scolding but she defended herself saying, "Well, she didn't seem to mind that much". The nurse apologised to me, but I had to laugh.

Weeks passed with the doctor eventually insisting a breast pump be applied to relieve me of some of the pain. I gasped in horror. The nurse very fortunately resisted him saying, "No, doctor, I just couldn't be so inhuman, it's agony for her already, she can't bear to be touched, never mind putting that thing on her". "All right", said the doctor, "I'll come again tomorrow and take her back to the nursing home as she obviously doesn't have scarlet fever". Minutes after arriving at the nursing home I was taken straight to the operating theatre, a mask planted over my face and told to breathe deeply. When I came round I found a tube and bandages adhering to my anatomy. Besides lancing and draining my breast abcess they told me my collapsed uterus now had a rubber ring supporting it. A rubber ring indeed. To me it felt more like a car tyre! I was so glad that abcess had been dealt with as never in my whole life have I spent eight weeks of such solid pain and misery. Thank goodness none of it could happen today. I've gone into detail to show just how crude medicine was even well into the present century. It was simply miraculous that we didn't contract diptheria or something else equally lethal in a situation where asepsis was virtually ignored.

So, after eight weeks, it turned out that Grandpa and I were released on the very same day, both of us weak and shaking from our experiences. How thankful we were to be back under Mrs. Dennis' wing, that dear kind soul at the pub, who helped us back to a full recovery.

CHAPTER 5

A South African Adventure

My first sea vogage. A succession of
awful nannies. Royal frolics

For a short while Grandpa was one of the young Surgeon Lieutenants attached to HMS St. Vincent, a boys training establisment. It's a wonder they ever got any volunteers at all, considering the harsh treatment the boys received, being flogged over a gymnasium "horse" just for being caught with a cigarette in their pocket when they were searched at the gates. This absolutely dreadful punishment had to be carried out in the presence of a doctor, often Grandpa. How many old retired sailors can remember going through such an ordeal as boys, I wonder. Even being searched when leaving the base to "go ashore" was, in itself, an indignity. More necessary now I'd say, with drugs not cigarettes being sought. Today's youth seem to need firm discipline far more so than then, but unhappily don't seem to get it.

Learning about naval etiquette, the "do's and don'ts" expected of me, was quite a trial. I had to attend and watch football and rugby matches, try to look intelligent and applaud appropriately when everyone else did, even though I hadn't a clue about what was going on. I've never enjoyed watching sport, finding it a real bore. Once, appearing at "The Match" for Grandpa's sake, I whispered to him, "I expect they'll have to stop now the ball's got damaged". "What do you mean?", he asked. "Well look", I said, "It's gone a funny pointed shape". After furtive glances all around to ensure that no-one had heard my asinine remark, he hissed, "Be quiet, you nit! It's not football they're playing. It's rugger!" After that I was careful not to come out with any more remarks. What I didn't understand, I kept quiet about.

In less than three months we were on the move again. Appointed to HMS Harebell, a fishing protection vessel, Grandpa sailed off leaving three month old Jill and me in a tiny but adequate bungalow at Weymouth. We'd spent a bad fortnight in the Portland Station Hotel before finding this, a grim memory of poor food, and stifling smoke — we walked about outside with Jill, for fear she would choke. Mother came to Weymouth and helped me look after the baby whom she adored. When Grandpa came home on leave there were some scenes as Mother's ideas about the baby's care and his didn't always coincide. I wasn't even consulted of course.

Thirteen months later I moved with my bouncing rosy cheeked healthy baby to a flat in Highgate, London, together with a very nice maid I'd acquired. She enjoyed life in London, flirting with all the tradesmen and making friends with maids in other flats, one day insisting I went down to look at an enormous fish she'd seen in the flat occupied by the Jewish owner of the whole building. To my surprise, this creature was swimming around alive in the bath! It was simply huge! I'd never seen anything like it before. Seemingly, its a Jewish custom and would later finish up in a special "stew".

This was yet another temporary residence though for in less than six months, off we went to the Cape of Good Hope, South Africa, with a posting to Simonstown Naval Hospital. How exciting! I'd never travelled on a liner before, and found the prospect thrilling. The old "Garth Castle" on which we travelled took three weeks getting there. Being only twenty two I never tired of dancing through the night and playing all the games and sports. I was truly sad when all this high living came to a halt at the end of the voyage. A whole new life awaited me though, and I soon fell in love with South Africa.

That journey on the Garth Castle gave me my first taste of what life on board a liner was really like. It happened to be the smallest ship I was ever to travel on, except for the Chinese coastal steamers which were a different matter altogether. Our

April 1930 (1st Liner I ever sailed in)

MENU

UNION-CASTLE LINE

S.S. "GARTH CASTLE"

Commander . . . . H. L. SCHOLEFIELD

FIRST SALOON

DINNER.

Hors d'Œuvre
Consommé Profiterole
Potage Chesterfield
Poached Turbot, Richelieu
Médaillons of Turkey, Supreme
Sea Kale au Jus
Quarter Lamb, Mint Sauce
Potatoes : Château, Boiled
Cauliflower
Larded Pheasant, Anglaise
Salads : Plain and Demi-deuil

Sweets
Pouding Denmark
Coupe St. Jose
Sponge Fingers

Savoury
Prawn Curry

Cheese
Dessert   Coffee

April 24th, 1931

SMOKING IS NOT PERMITTED IN THE SALOON.

ROMEO & JULIET

WILL OWEN

fellow passengers became so well known to us that by the end of the trip they had become old friends. I was introduced to the unique "crossing the line" ceremony, on this trip when we crossed the equator. In this rowdy affair, anyone who's not crossed the equator before gets a most wild and enthusiastic dunking in the swimming pool. Firstly though they're thoroughly covered from head to middle in shaving soap, whilst everyone aboard watches and laughs. Luckily it only seemed to apply to the men, for I confess I'd have hated going through the ordeal myself. I didn't escape being threatened with it and teased though!

We always knew if we were sailing anywhere near land even if it wasn't visible by the sea birds that appeared. They would follow us, hovering above our heads to accept anything we might throw to them. I saw my first albatross on this trip. The size of these birds took my breath away, having a wing span that seemed to spread from one side of the ship to the other. Utterly enormous, they seem quite unafraid of anyone. Fortunately at the time I hadn't yet heard of the tragedy of a certain trawler skipper. This seafarer had often taken his little two year old son with him. One day the child fell though the rails into the sea and before he could be rescued an albatross got him. Hearing this tale put a very different light on these magnificent birds, with their gorgeous wings but cruel beaks. I can understand why the bereaved skipper said he would have no hesitation in shooting down any he clapped eyes on in cold blood, as the very name of the bird brought back the horror of his tragic loss.

Arriving at Capetown, we were met by several naval colleagues and driven to a very well known hotel in Simonstown called the Lord Nelson. I'm sure that the entire Navy knows of this establishment as just about everyone arriving in Capetown stayed there, as did we. After about a month we moved into our freshly painted house. Now, there began a hectic life of such social activity that, looking back on it, I wonder we didn't die of exhaustion. But, firstly, a nanny had to be found for Jill. Other naval wives smugly told me I should have brought one with me from England as they had. As it turned out they were wrong, as all of their nannies were sent back for disgraceful behaviour. I must say I didn't fare any better though, having to endure a succession of total failures.

I failed to check the first one's references. A pity, for this local convent girl proved to be a thief and was flung out after a month at a minutes notice, her irate mother appearing on my doorstep within an hour. To detail all that girl's antics would fill a book. By now Jocelyn had arrived, being born at our home after the then customary three weeks in bed without so much as a toe touching the ground. A nurse attended me superbly for six weeks thereafter. Jocelyn arrived at five past eleven on a glorious June morning, June 9th 1932, a most lovely, wide awake little soul, with enormous blue eyes.

By telephoning a Capetown agency I found a new nanny, a highly qualified Princess Christian trained nurse, claiming to be middle aged with excellent references. On her arrival she seemed rather older than I'd expected and, when I asked her age, she just said, very abruptly, "Oh, middle-aged". She seemed at least sixty, being a fierce tall and forbidding looking red haired Scotswoman, with a very high opinion of herself to boot. But, being so well qualified and experienced I felt we could leave the children in her care, even though we were out such a lot of the time. Soon, though, things started to make me wonder. On her second day, baking hot, she put the baby outside in her pram covered with several blankets and the hood up. Little Jocelyn's forehead was wet with perspiration. Tentatively, I asked, "Nanny, do you think baby's rather hot, could we perhaps have the hood down?" But all I got in reply, with great dignity, was, "I've been looking after children since before you were born, I don't need any advice now, thank you!" Chastened, I crept inside, sat down and thought, "What have I got!" To say she was a real dragon was putting it mildly! I lost a stone in weight while she was with me and I was scared stiff of her. Two male friends who called, she chased off, despite my protestations, claiming they'd woken the baby up, which they hadn't. I'd seen Jocelyn contentedly examining her little hands in her pram on the verandah, and I had readily agreed when they asked if they could look at her, as their wives were expecting children themselves.

The "Dragon" even objected when I suggested taking two and a half year old Jill to the beach with me, thinking it would be a bit of a help while baby had her bath. This brought the retort, "You take that child, you can keep her, I shall completely wash my hands of her — you can do the washing, the lot". I was speechless. Jill, hearing this, piped up, "I want to go to the beach with Mummy". Swiftly I was told, "Take the spoilt brat then. I've said all I'm going to". With which the nursery door was slammed in my face. Jocelyn didn't thrive as we wished or seem to be gaining any weight. Weekly, some scales were brought up from the chemist, for nanny to use behind the closed nursery doors. Grandpa pressed me to find out what was happening, saying it was my job to sort things out with the woman — he wouldn't interfere. So, the next time the scales came I went to the nursery to be met with, "What are you here for?" I said, "I've come to see baby weighed." About to go on the scales, Jocelyn was lying naked on the Dragon's lap. Sinking back into her chair she told me, "Well then, I shan't weigh her while you're here." At this I snapped, "Right!", and picking up the scales retored, "I'll send them back and weigh her when you're not around." On and on it went. She'd pass me in the corridor, head held high, a tray of baby food aloft and never utter a word. I confided to cook, who hated her as well, that I couldn't stand it much longer. I tried telling Grandpa, but all he would say was, "Oh, you women must settle it between yourselves." Finally came the last straw and Grandpa was driven to take action. He heard himself how Nanny went in to Jocelyn and deliberately woke her up to give her a feed much before the right time, just so she could get to bed early herself. This had become a regular occurrence. "Right", said Grandpa, "I'll deal with that bitch!" Upstairs he went and I heard no end of raised voices with Grandpa finishing up saying, "You'll be out of the house tomorrow at nine sharp or your bags will be out in the road." I was overjoyed but scared to be there when she left, so having warned cook what I was doing, rushed off with Jill early next morning to a friends, later phoning to see if the dragon had gone. Cook told me, "She's gone Madam, you can come home now". It was one of the happiest days of my life when she left.

On the few occasions the dragon did condescend to talk to me at all, the conversation would always be about how she'd brought up Lady Cunard's children and how she used to take them to tea with the Duke of Windsor. So it wasn't difficult to hazard a guess at how old she really was. It worked out to be over 60! It later transpired that we hadn't been the only ones to suffer. The same cavalier treatment had been accorded to her previous employers, who'd been landed with some substantial hotel bills

False Bay, Simonstown, South Africa. Photographed by Grandpa from near the Naval Sanatorium. A railway followed the coastline to finish up at Capetown. The Naval Dockyard is at the right, and the training ship Botha moored left centre.

Our First South African House. During our
first visit, 1931-34 we lived at Sunnyside.

incurred on their behalf, but without their knowledge. Of course
I knew none of this before I engaged her.

In the short three years we were at Simonstown we met
many interesting people. The much feted Amy Johnson, for
instance, who had just completed her famous flight. The late
Duke of Kent, paid his memorable visit to South Africa whilst we
were there. Not at all like the splendid and delightful person his
son, the present Duke, I feel its better not to dwell much on that
visit. The only resemblanc between the two of them for me is
purely one of features, stature and build. Suffice it to say that
when I met the late Duke at a small private Admiralty House
dance, his hands shook badly, one trusted from the strain of his
engagements and not excessive celebrations or indulgences. At
the same function he seemed to have difficulty in getting his
partners around the dance floor frequently needing to depart
into the gardens with them for fresh air. On their return it
appeared that several of these ladies had needed to help him
physically, their dresses and composure being noticeably
disturbed. I myself had to comfort and help at least one of his
consorts that evening, effecting running repairs to her broken
shoulder straps. Perhaps the strain of his many engagements,
often going on to the early hours, had produced a pallor, needing
to be disguised by the application of what seemed to be

quantities of cosmetics, rather than other possibly more fanciful explanations put forward at the time, and since.

We became quite friendly with several of the Duke's A.D.C.'s, who told us many tales of his activities, including what can only be called a vigorous night life, which often reduced his entourage to complete exhaustion. Once, the Duke became bored with the Caledonian Ball given in his honour in Capetown and commanded that a special dance be set up in the middle of the night at Admiralty House, Simonstown. This necessitated turning out the band from HMS Cardiff, and waking up half the tradespeople in Simonstown to lay on all the refreshments, to everyones annoyance.

We had been warned H.R.H. would never dream of going to bed before 4.30 a.m. any day, his ADC's finding this pretty enervating, not being exactly young men. On the night of the Admiralty House Ball, although no one is supposed to leave before Royalty, the C. in C. gave us permission to go early (at three o'clock), telling me, "Certainly, my dear, you go home — H.R.H. is in no condition to know whether anyone has left or not."

This most charming, lively, C. in C. was E.R.G.R. Evans. Evans of the "Broke" later to become Lord Mountevans, the same Evans who had been in the Scott Expedition to the Antartic. A small stocky man in extreme contrast to his lovely, blond, but very large Norwegian wife. He told me himself that he met her, proposed and was accepted all within the space of two hours! No one could be very formal in his company, and many were the happy parties we had at Admiralty House often with wild after-dinner games.

I owed much hospitality to many of the senior ranks and their wives, particularly our own Seniors, Surgeon Commander and Mrs. Twigg, who lived in a house up the hill from us. Little did I know, we were to occupy that very house ourselves many years later. Mrs. Twigg kept her critical eye on me pretty well, pulling me up if I failed to return someone's phone call, or commenting unfavourably if perhaps one day I'd omitted to put on any stockings. I suppose I tried to dodge her really, not liking this treatment. Although we regarded the Twigg's as friends, one was still careful not to overstep the mark. To return the Twigg's and others hospitality I knew I would have to give a small dinner party myself. It turned out to be one of those occasions, when no matter how important it is that all goes well, contrarily everything that can go wrong, does. I can laugh at it now but I didn't at the time.

I chose the ten guests, not counting ourselves, with much forethought, including just a few junior couples to brighten up the occasion. As the Twigg's would be there, to say I prepared it all most carefully is putting it mildly. I knew Mrs. Twigg would be most critical, and anything she found out of order would be discussed in depth by all and sundry. I decided we'd have chicken as the main course, being an uncommon dish and quite a delicacy then, rather than commonplace fillet steak or beef. The evening began badly as I'd had a foul sore throat and temperature all day that I knew I'd have to disguise 'till the party was over. When all but two of our guests had arrived, it slowly dawned on me that this couple, a young marine and his wife, might have forgotten all about it. "But maybe they've had an accident," I thought, "I'd better phone". No, they'd forgotten alright. They were horrified and so was I, for it upset my seating arrangements. Hastily I told them not to worry, put the phone down, and quickly got the kitchen staff to remove two chairs and place settings. Ready to start the meal at last we all filed in to begin what was to be a fiasco from start to finish. For a start I discovered that the man I had engaged to wait on the table was quite drunk. I couldn't believe my eyes for he was well known and well used by the Naval community, but drunk he unmistakably was. Too much so, I'm afraid, to hope that no one would notice. The main course arrived, Grandpa getting up to carve the chickens on the sideboard. As he stuck his fork into the first one, it skidded off the dish and to my dismay flew right across the room. Next a messenger arrived calling Grandpa to the hospital to sew up a badly cut rating, who was bleeding profusely. He disappeared at once, the dinner continuing without him. The next course, the sweet, (as I thought), was now being served. Chattering away busily, to my mortification I suddenly noticed "drunky" was serving the savoury! He didn't see my signal though, and by the time I'd got through to him half the guests had their plates of savoury before them. He promptly whipped away the plates from under their noses and brought in the sweets. Eventually when dinner was over, and the ladies were esconced in the drawing room for coffee, who should burst in but a very breathless and apologetic marine and his wife. At that stage they couldn't have been less welcome; I was obliged to explain to everyone what had happened. I dare say it all sounds trivial now, but then it seemed a total disaster. I'm glad to say that nothing like it ever happened to me again. That night though I reckon my luck was clean out.

My Nanny problems after the "Dragon" had gone continued

for yet another month. I told the agency what I thought of them, concluding with a very positive instruction to send someone younger than myself. What did I get? A woman they described as "just perfect, excellent references and credentials etc.", but they feared she was in her forties albeit cheerful and active etc. Quite in despair as I had no one else in view, I took her on. She arrived and seemed all they had told me but curiously left all her luggage in the downstairs storeroom, saying that she could, "unpack it later at my leisure". A pleasant month later she left giving me one day's notice. I was astonished, as everything had seemed very satisfactory. It appeared that not only did all her friends live in Capetown, something I'd wondered about, but she'd had a job to go to all along, merely filling in the spare month by coming to me! She sent me some staggering taxi bills which she'd run up getting back from Simonstown, taking taxis just to avoid getting wet when it came on to rain! Once she even commandeered a dockyard lorry to get the pram home! Nappies I found bore unmistakable signs of uses other than for which they were intended. Disgusted, I burnt the lot. Fuming, I told the agency what I thought of them. I must have got through at long last or maybe I was just lucky for now they sent me a dear, capable, partly Dutch, very blond girl of twenty nine, who served us well to the end of our stay. Both the children and I loved her, and I begged her to come back home with us. She wouldn't, though. Coming from the country, she was a real home bird, who wouldn't leave her parents, so, with much reluctance, we had to part company. Losing her, and about to go home I felt that a wonderful time was ending, although I knew there would be lots more in the future. When we got to England I could only reflect on all the joys of sun, grapes, beach parties, and friends I'd left behind. In fact I was quite homesick for the Cape, never realising I was to be there again years later.

CHAPTER 6

Back to England for Three Years

*A fabulous voyage, Alverstoke, Dulwich
and Oriel Cottage. School begins for the
children*

We came back home to England in the Llangibby Castle during
the early spring of 1934, having had a most magnificent send off
from Capetown complete with all our many friends, press
photographers, reporters and so on. I've still got press photos of
the occasion showing everybody, including Nanny, and Mrs.
Bull, a very special friend of ours. Dr. Bull, our own family doctor,
and his wife had lived in Simonstown for many years, having
come there from Scotland. Although a most lovable pair, quite
devoted to each other, nevertheless now and then one of them
would drop in alone. We would enquire, "Where's Margaret (or
Pop)?", and whichever one had come would answer, "Oh, we
had a Bull fight this morning, so I've no idea!" We kept in touch
through succeeding years, and they stayed with us in London in
1954.

Having said our farewells, we settled down for yet another
fabulous sea trip on the Llangibby, calling at Madeira, Ascension
Island and St. Helena. Anchoring a couple of miles from the
shore of barren Ascension, we passed some time throwing
loaves to absolute hoards of fish that leapt and fought each other

alongside the ship. These they greedily demolished quicker than I can write this down. Soon we spied several small boats coming out to us loaded with the biggest turtles I've ever seen. These poor clumsy helpless creatures were unceremoniously dumped alive onto part of the partially flooded lower deck. All the children on board, including mine, rushed down below to inspect them, and sit on their backs! To this day, I've got a photo of Jill astride one of the unfortunate animals. It seems these turtles were being sent to England specially to be served up at the Lord Mayor of London's banquet as real turtle soup. This tradition was observed every year, a cargo being sent annually at about this time for this purpose. I was sorry for them, knowing what their end was to be. Leaving the children on board with their Nanny, we went ashore at Madeira. An attractive place if you like hills for here these were terrific. Local chaps hauled us up one well known hill from the harbour on a sort of sledge on runners. Coming down was somewhat scary as if they'd let go, we should have developed an astonishing speed and finished up in the sea!

St. Helena was quite another matter. Although we'd never met him, the Governor, Sir Spencer Davis, gave us a lovely day with real V.I.P. treatmen. Hearing we were on board he sent his launch out to take us off, to transfer on landing to the official chauffeur driven Daimler for a tour of the island. The chief attraction was the house where Emperor Napoleon had spent his exile. I was fascinated to see that it had been left, or arranged, to remain as nearly as possible as it had been during his occupation, even to his cup and saucer and all the bathroom and toilet articles being in place. Our tour round finished up at Government House where we had a luxurious lunch, Sir Spencer being a most charming host. Afterwards he took us over his beautiful grounds, asking if we had enjoyed our day. We certainly had. A truly memorable, beautiful day.

The rest of the voyage home went off as it usually did. Games and swimming all day, eating, chatting with everyone, and then baths, which were always announced with a respectful, "Your bath is ready, Madam". Choosing which of my many lovely evening gowns I'd wear that night came next, followed by dinner and dancing into the small hours.

Arriving home in early April, we went to the Angelsey Hotel in Alverstoke, mother arriving to greet her second grandchild, 22 month old Jocelyn, for the first time. Being biased, perhaps I shouldn't say it but she was a lovely child, more like a delicate little china doll though than her sturdy older sister, always the

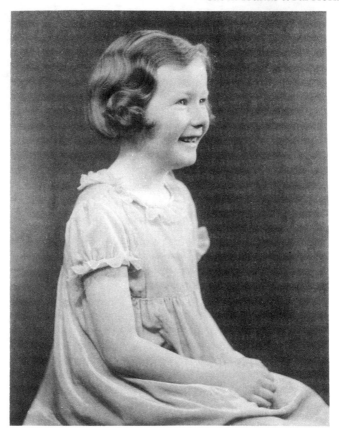

Jill: Jill Blundstone Hodgson neé Pomfret —
b. 21st September 1929, my elder daughter
aged 5.

more boisterous of the two. Even then there was a very deep and
close companionship between the two, strengthening over the
years, affording me infinite happiness.

In those days to be without a Nanny was quite unthinkable.
Before leaving South Africa I'd had no difficulty in finding a
most capable gentle spinster of thirty five, who obviously adored
children, to accompany us back to England. She seemed reliable,
and was willing to come with us, perhaps to stay in the U.K. for
some years. Although a quite delightful person, I suspected

"Joc": Jocelyn Leslie Blundstone Boswell neé
Pomfret — b. 9th June 1932 (in S. Africa), my
younger daughter aged 3.

she'd be unsuitable for life in England, having been waited on all
her life up to then. One day, for example, she diffidently asked
me if she'd be expected to wash her own underwear and
stockings! Confirming this, I pointed out that life in England
nowadays didn't include nannies being waited on like that.

After only a week in the Hotel at Alverstoke, the
proprietoress spoke to me, firmly announcing she couldn't
tolerate Nanny upsetting the staff any longer. My heart sank. "In
what way?", I asked. It seemed she spent much of her time in the

lounge talking with the older, snobby, residents. The servants were treated contemptuously, when they brought in her morning tea tray. She was quite above cleaning the children's shoes, putting these outside the door to be done. Generally she adopted all sorts of airs and graces, when, as the hotel staff pointed out, she was really only a servant like they were after all. To cap it all, she'd used up all the hotel notepaper! All of this saddened me. Tactfully, I told Nanny that attitudes had changed in England and this behaviour must stop. Soon afterwards she left.

We moved around a lot in 1934. From the Alverstoke Hotel the children and I went to a bungalow in Privett Road, Alverstoke whilst Grandpa was away on a short course in London. Life went on smoothly for five months, mother coming to stay with us for a while. Next, we moved to a house in Dulwich Village, London. Jill livened up the unexciting time there by setting fire to the fireside seats, flames spreading up the curtains before I got there and quenched the conflagration. I had daily help in the person of a very dim-witted middle aged spinster who couldn't be trusted to do anything right, not even make a milk pudding! The only notable events I recall happening was a spate of eight burglaries, all within five months, up and down our long road which stretched from East Dulwich to Dulwich Village. Pyjama clad, a neighbour went downstairs one night to get a cup of tea surprising an intruder emptying his cupboards of silver and cutlery. The intruder fled, the neighbour giving chase, his cries of, "Help!", "Thief!", "Stop!", waking us all up. Police said another, better planned, burglary was of a familiar pattern. One member of a gang who had found details of an affluent wedding from the press obtained employment with the newly weds as a maid. Finding her to be efficient and reliable, she was left in sole charge, whilst they were out one night. Quickly apprising her conspirators, a furniture van was conjured up, the whole house being emptied of valuables and furniture, with their activities shielded by a fortuitous fog. Oddly, that night, Grandpa and I were returning from seeing a film at a local cinema, and were walking to our house from the bus stop. We actually saw the van, but it didn't strike us as strange that people were apparently moving out during the night, though, as even then nothing that happened in London could ever really surprise me.

Jill's schooldays began whilst we were in Dulwich, her first nursery school being the same one Stanley Lupino, a famous music hall artist, had attended as a small child. Life was so different from South Africa, with no parties, except one very elaborate ball in the Painted Hall at Greenwich, and not much to do at all. I passed the time taking Jocelyn in a pushchair round the parks, feeding ducks and skimming stones across the frozen pond until a park keeper stopped me with a severe reprimand. It seemed the pond was used for ice skating, and stones on the ice constituted a danger to the skaters.

Soon we were back in Alverstoke at Oriel Cottage in St. Mark's Row with Grandpa appointed to the R.N. Hospital, Haslar, and for the next three years my life was very happy indeed.

I'd brought a girl with me from London who proved to be a first class cook. A very doleful soul of twenty five, she never wanted to go out and have any fun, probably because her parents were strict Plymouth Bretheren. I thought, "I'll soon settle that! When she makes a few friends with some sailor boys it'll be quite another matter." And so it was. Gradually she thawed out, telling me, "You know, Madam, it's you who've set me on the downward path", which I took as a compliment! Her "downward path" had, after all, only meant going to cinemas and dances with a few friends. Unfortunately she became rather choosey not wishing to wash out tea towels saying that so and so's maid had told her all theirs went to the laundry. Seeing her ironing an attractive petticoat one day that wasn't mine prompted me to enquire where she'd got it. Her answer rather stunned me. "Actually Madam", she told me, "It isn't mine, I'm doing it for a friend whose mistress won't let her use an electric iron". I took a very dim view of this, stopping her doing it in the future. Eventually she left us, someone having tempted her away with more money. After she left I was able to replace her with Patricia, a real gem who cooked equally well, and who got on with our new nanny famously.

Both Jill and Jocelyn were now going to a little private school literally just across the road run by two sweet elderly sisters called the Misses King. The cook there, Mrs. Lane, let me know that her daughter, Doris, loved children and was looking for a job. Meeting her I knew that I'd found exactly what I wanted. She was very young, always beautifully groomed in her striped uniform with its starched collar, very sweet and an absolute darling. I took her on as nanny and she stayed with us until we went off to the Far East. Years later it grieved me to hear that she'd worked on the buses during the war and had contracted T.B. Meeting her only once again, I learned she'd married, but with one lung gone and the other badly affected, her expectation of life was very poor, her doctor not allowing her to have any children. I would love to know what eventually happened to her as she was far too nice to ever forget.

Oriel Cottage was furnished very nicely and had polished parquet floors. With so much help it was easily kept quite spotless. One day Nanny took me into the drawing room to show me something, pausing at the door to say, "Madam, please don't be cross". "Whatever is it, Nanny?", I asked. She just pointed to the bay windows with their heavy green curtains. Each had been cut nearly right across about two feet from the ground, the strips trailing on the floor. Aghast as they weren't mine, I gasped, "They're ruined! Who did it?" No answer. Then it dawned on me who it might be. "Jocelyn", I called, "Come here, I want to speak to you". She came in and answering my, "Did you do this Jocelyn?", the tiny blue eyed innocent calmly replied, "Yes, Mummy, I did." I was completely floored. I said I was shocked and horrified and a lot of other things, finishing up with, "And to think that a schoolgirl could do such a senseless thing." Straight back she came back at me with, "Oh, I did that yesterday Mummy, and I wasn't a schoolgirl then because I only started school today." She was right, too. The curtains were repaired with hours of painstaking darning, making them passably presentable, although I expect we paid for the damage in full at the end of our stay there.

The girls shared a bedroom together at Oriel Cottage, and as children will at that age, frequently demanded my attention. I was downstairs in the lounge one evening after they had gone to bed. They had a disagreement over something or other, the first I knew of it being when Jill called down to me, "Mummy, Mummy, come up, come up here". Having been dragged upstairs like this on rather too many occasions for my liking I called back with some asperity, "What is it now", whilst starting up the stairs. "Do you know what Jocelyn's just said to me Mummy?", came the reply. "Of course I don't", I answered back, "What did she say? Tell me." Jocelyn, quite exasperated with Jill over something had terminated the exchange with the rudest remark she could think of, for Jill reported, "Mummy, Jocelyn said 'Oh, bare botties to you anyway, Jill'." Perhaps they remember the incident. I wonder.

Mrs. Thornton came into our lives around this time, initially to take charge of everything whilst I went to a London Nursing Home to have some internal adjustments carried out, a legacy of Jocelyn's birth. I was soon back home but she was so good that I kept her, on a half daily basis, in addition to the others. Grandpa was away quite a lot often sleeping at Haslar whilst on duty. I suppose Mrs. Thornton was more of a companion than anything else. A marvellous seamstress, she turned out some beautiful clothes for the children, making them frocks, panties, bonnets and sun outfits. Always, I dressed them alike. They looked utterly lovely, quite adorable, in their pretty liberty prints. I couldn't help loving Mrs. Thornton, she was such a lively bubbling person with a tremendous enthusiasm for life. Her husband must have been very tolerant, for he never objected to her staying with me till 11 p.m. when Grandpa was away, laughing, gossiping, sewing and trying on clothes. Now aged ninety, she lives in Canada, near her only daughter and family. We became firm friends and correspond nostalgically to this day, recalling those happy times in the mid thirties.

Grandpa deluded himself all his life that he was an expert on everything, particularly plumbing. Eventually I was reduced to begging everyone to say nothing if something went wrong, some frightful situations having arisen as the result of his efforts.

Once he had cook in hysterics with the kitchen floor deep in hot water. I've seen water cascading out of upstairs tanks. Then the bathroom washbasin got blocked. He couldn't undo the trap, so, having a brain wave, went to work on it with an enema tube to try to "pump" it out, but the nozzle came off and got stuck. So off he went to Haslar leaving us to summon a plumber to sort things out. I made myself scarce saying "I'm going out, I'm not facing him when he finds out what's in there!" The plumber was indeed very curious and puzzled, as naturally he would be, Nanny trying to explain to him what had happened.

Rather unfortunately the lease on our house expired three months before we were due to leave England. Luckily we found another one, to tide us over, only six doors away down the road. The move didn't cause as much upset as it might, except Grandpa said there was no way he would leave five hundredweights of coal behind. Then he demanded everyones help to shift it. Quite rightly, both Nanny and Cook flatly refused, so that left me! An old rickety pram was pressed into use for the filthy job. Somebody we knew might see us, I protested. What would we look like pushing an old pram filled with coal? My objections were overruled of course, and work commenced, Cook and Nanny peeping at us around the gate. Just as I'd anticipated, a car came past us with a Haslar doctor and his family inside, all waving like mad and laughing their heads off, with us, by now, as black as colliers. It didn't bother Grandpa one bit. All his life he made his own rules and couldn't care less what anyone thought.

CHAPTER 7

An Ocean Voyage to Paradise Island, Liukungtao

Eventually, after three good years, we heard our next posting was to be to Wei-Hai-Wei in the China Staion, so all the many preparations to leave England got under way once again.

October, when we were due to leave, was getting closer, and our Morris Oxford, old when we got it, was sold to a friend for ten pounds. All the floorboards were loose and could be taken up at will. Just as well, for once I'd left Grandpa with Jocelyn in the car, whilst I took Jill into Boots at Gosport to change a book in the lending library they had in those days. Coming back Jill said, "Look, Mummy, there's water pouring out underneath the car". And so it was — a puddle was spreading out from under the car in all directions. Jocelyn, then two or three years old, had been "caught short" and wanted to "spend a penny". With nowhere handy, Grandpa had taken up a floor board to make a very handy, useful outlet.

Eventually, the day to set off on our 9000 mile journey to the Orient arrived. Most of our belongings had gone on ahead, including a bicycle I'd paid thirty bob for (one pound fifty pence), taken on the advice that it would be useful there, which indeed it was. Grandpa supervised the loading of our taxi, our personal cases being fitted inside and strapped on the back, amid many heated words between Grandpa and the driver. Always early, we were first on the Portsmouth ferry, and so first off, with a long queue of cars, vans and lorries behind us. The tide was out, and as we trundled up the steep and slippery ramp, there was a sudden yell, and much commotion. Looking behind I saw our cases sliding off, bursting open, my hairbrush, make-up case, teddy bears — oh, just dozens of personal things — slithering towards the edge of the slimy slipway. Grandpa and the driver leapt out and rushed around trying to collect everything, to an accompaniment of much horn honking by all the other drivers, irritated by the hold up. Jill shouted, "Oh, Mummy, look! All our things are going!" "No, I don't want to look, I just can't bear it", I murmured. Anyway, I was so tightly wedged in with five year old Jocelyn, eight year old Jill and so many bags and cases that I couldn't have got out to help even if I'd wanted to. Everything was eventually collected and our long and tiresome journey to Birkenhead continued. We sailed for the Far East on the Steamship Patroclus, a comparatively small vessel by the usual standards, to be our temporary home for the next few weeks until we arrived at Shanghai.

I've always enjoyed life on board ship. On this trip we had an absolutely first class cabin steward, a North Country fellow who just couldn't do enough for us. Never having travelled by air I really don't know what it's like. Surely, though, it can't compare with the beauty of several weeks at sea, making friends, having fun and having attention lavished on one day and night. To be truly spoilt, even to having hot soup or ice cream, depending on the weather, being brought to one's chair each day at 11.00 each morning. We swam every day, played games and sports, and were fascinated by the schools of porpoise and spouting whales. Some of the many flying fish landed on deck, to be cooked for breakfast next day. Leaning over the rail on hot moonlight nights to watch the trails of phosphorescence alongside was sheer magic. Music, dancing, cocktail parties, fancy dress nights, oh, how can all this be compared with a flight, over in a few hours, never having had to leave one's seat or been able to get to know other passengers. I'm so glad, oh, so glad I've lived in other times and was young when lifestyle was at its very best, with an easy, uncrowded, unhurried and unpressurised day-to-day existence. For me, to have been in my teens in the twenties was the most fortunate thing that could have ever happened to me.

Our trip out to the Far East took several weeks, by way of the Mediterranean, Suez Canal and the Indian Ocean. We spent a day at Marseilles, our first port of call, where we toured round in a taxi taking in the sights. One particular sight specially intrigued the two girls, and me too for that matter, were the extraordinary gents loos dotted around the town. Their very open, almost skeleton construction, allowed the men to walk in, stand still for a while, and then walk out the other side as if nothing had happened! As they stood there, we could see them

T.S.S. "PATROCLUS"
Commander   W. Maclure

**Children's Tea
Party**

Thursday, 18th November, 1937

CHILDREN

:-: **T E A** :-:

Miss Jean Brodie

Master John Coleman-Doscas

Miss Elizabeth Coleman-Doscas

Master Michael Dugran

Master Henry Hilton

Miss Linette Hilton

Miss Deldre Hurd-Wood

Miss Jennifer Ingram

Master Rowan Menzies

Miss Liliane Moxon

Master John Penn

Miss Pat Penn

Miss Jill Pomfret

Miss Jocelyne Pomfret

Fried Fillet Plaice

Minced Capon

Lamb Cutlets & Green Peas
Mashed Potatoes

Eggs;-Boiled, Poached, Scrambled
Omelettes:-Plain, Tomato, Confiture

Cold
York Ham   Galantine of Turkey
Salad

Milk Jelly   Lemon Ices
Strawberries & Cream

Rainbow Cake

Tea   Cocoa

perfectly from waist up and also below mid thigh. It soon dawned on me what was happening, but not of course to my intensely observant and curious daughters. It had to be explained to them!

By now the Patroclus felt like our own home, and we were always glad to get back on board to greet our friends and exchange experiences. There were lots of children on board, Jill and Jocelyn soon making many friends. Although the children had separate meal times and menus, mothers and nannies would assemble with them to see what their young ones would be having. Meals were most elaborate in contrast to the nursery meals to which they were accustomed. My two quickly got used to choosing from a menu, so much so that years later just after arriving in Bermuda Jocelyn inadvertently gave me a good laugh. For the first time in years we were in an ordinary bungalow of our own and having to fend for ourselves. Sitting down to our first homely meal she quite politely and innocently enquired, "Can I see the menu please, Mummy?" Laughingly, I replied, "Oh no my dear, this is it. No choice while we live here, I can assure you". The meals on the Patroclus were fully up to the standard of the usual meals on board ship. Simply superb. After my usual four days flat on my back hoping to die, I recovered slowly to enjoy the rest of the trip to the full. I'll always remember the dainty chicken sandwiches our lovely steward brought me, trying to tempt me to eat during those early days, when even the sound of the dinner gong was enough to turn my stomach over. Jill wasn't much better, but Jocelyn for some reason wasn't affected on either this or other occasions.

Port Said was our next stop, with shopping and lunch ashore with Naval friends. As usual in those days, the "gully gully" men came on board with their entertainment of snakes, birds, conjuring tricks etc., which the children adored. And of course no end of tradesmen with baskets full of silks, embroideries, linens, hats and novelties. They practically fought each other in attempting to gain our attention. All was noise, excitement and bustle. This turbulent crowd had to be almost shovelled off the ship by force before we could sail again. Going through the Suez Canal was as exciting as it had been promised to be. Or at least the first stage was. We lined the rails as the ship edged along, watching teams of camels on the banks seemingly only touching distance away. There we were enjoying all of this tremendously, when along came Grandpa. It was 6 o'clock, the time for the children's bath. And he wasn't going to have their routine upset, Suez Canal or no Suez Canal. To my intense chagrin, we had to leave this fascinating scene to attend to this mundane but apparently essential task, followed of course by their evening meal. I was extremely cross about this, and didn't hesitate to say so. Of course his fanatical attitude over punctuality was well known. Although I agree it's very important most of the time, on this occasion I felt it was unnecessary and very unthinking of him not to stretch a point. Generally speaking, it seems to me that punctuality is synonymous with reliability. I wish it was an inherited attribute, as indeed it is, on at least the female side of our family.

Through the searing heat of the Indian Ocean to Columbo came next. Here we went out to the naval base to spend a day with Paymaster Commander Stapley and his wife. We bathed in a sea so tepid that it must have been at air temperature. Afterwards our hosts showed us the huge newly constructed dry dock. As I stood on its edge I'd have welcomed falling in, such a raging headache I'd got from the stifling heat. Sadly we bade them farewell. It would have been sadder still had we known that our delightful and congenial host would soon be posted back to

England to be killed on active duty.

The next leg of our voyage took us across the Bay of Bengal and the Andaman Sea to Penang, our next refuelling station. This operation took several days as ours was a coal burning ship, oil fired liners yet to come into service. As far as possible everything in our cabins had to be covered, for layers of coal dust settled on everything. All day and night the local coolies ran up and down the gangways laden with sacks of coal across their shoulders for but a pittance of money. In spite of the meagre pay there was no shortage of labour as this was just about the only way the coolies could make a living, if that's what one could call it. Penang fascinated me. I'd never before been in the wonderful temples found there, or seen the religious rites that go on within. Much was explained to us about all the activities, with the monks placing dishes of strange looking food before the altars, and ringing of bells. All this coupled with the incense smoke created a really weird atmosphere. I've never climbed so many steps, or seen so many snakes writhing in open pools surrounded by exotic flowers and plants. Of course, everything had some religious meaning. It seems a pity their religion didn't extend to doing something about the innumerable and shockingly crippled beggars who lined the stone steps everywhere, with hands outstretched pleading for anything anyone would give. It tore at my heart to see these blind, limbless skeletons, barely alive, all about, while food was being offered up in the temples to their particular gods. Walking through the streets at sundown was a particularly harrowing experience. Having gone once I refused to go again. Inert forms lay everywhere in huddled heaps, so many that one even had to step right over them. One couldn't have been blamed for thinking they were dead bodies. They were either dead asleep, dead drunk or dead drugged. Mostly the latter, I was informed. I found the spectacle quite shattering. Perhaps though, in their condition, they didn't have to put up with so called life much longer. With so much deprivation and degradation everywhere, it was unsurprising that we were warned to lock our cabin doors and portholes securely before going ashore. Horrific tales abounded of unspeakable crimes, all true no doubt, so we needed no second warning. In essence, Penang is a truly beautiful tropical dream. Why has mankind defiled it so? Reflecting on this trip, the first but longest we made, I feel so very grateful that I have been able to see so much of this lovely world, and to see it when I did. Fifty years later, I'm still entranced by the memory of all the beautiful places I was privileged to visit. Thankfully, many aspects of life

which I found so distressing have now been much improved.

Passing down the Straits of Malacca we proceeded to Singapore at the end of the Malay Peninsula. As hot as I'd expected, I went into the town well armed with aspirins. The Raffles Hotel I found intriguing. As usual we were met and taken on a round of sight seeing; but I never could enjoy such heat. Apart from all the exotic fruits and iced drinks I can't say I enjoyed it much. I enjoy it more now, as a memory. The whole trip out to the Far East was so lovely. Wherever we went, we were met by Naval personnel, who gave us star treatment. Even if we hadn't met our hosts before, it usually turned out that they would be great friends of someone we had met, sometime, somewhere. There was never any shortage of topics of conversation.

Hong Kong was next, another 1400 miles on across the South China Sea, and more refuelling. Up the famous peak we went in that unique tramway, clinging to the sides in a mixture of breathless apprehension and wide eyed wonder of the scenery. Near the top Jill spotted the Patroclus manoeuvring in the harbour, slowly edging away from the dockside. Crying out in tearful alarm she informed her father "Oh, Daddy, Daddy, they're going to sail without us!" We reassured her, still having another 800 miles to go to Shanghai, around the eastern coast of mainland China.

At last we reached our anchorage in the estuary off Shanghai. A river boat took us upstream, landing at the bank as I admired showers of brilliant fireworks cracking over our heads. Brisk voices urged us ashore though, and to take cover at once! They weren't fireworks at all, but anti-aircraft shells exploding — there was an air raid in progress! The Japanese, at war with China, were trying to bomb Shanghai. You can bet we hurried! A taxi took us as fast as possible to the Palace Hotel. This sticks in my mind chiefly as the place where I got my first taste of "Hongkong Dog" a vile tummy infection. I cleverly managed to catch 'flu at the same time and so felt pretty wretched.

It took five days on a small Chinese coastal steamer, the Shenking, to travel the last thousand miles to Wei-Hai-Wei. We were the only passengers, having to share a single cabin for four. By now it was December and we hadn't realised how bad the weather can be at that time of year. Soon enough we found out, being flung about like peas in a bottle, the ship pitching and rolling about so much that all we could do was cling to the sides of our bunks. I don't think I left mine once, except to go to the loo. People being sick all the time was a far from comforting sound. Poor Chinese people travelling with us in very uncomfortable conditions made ear splitting noises day and night with great abandon. Outside, snow was falling thick and fast, and great seas crashed against our porthole with such force I honestly thought the glass would smash. Day and night, armed guards, great hefty Russians, marched up and down past our porthole, smothered in furs and white with snow, heads bent against the blizzard, their faces practically invisible. Enquiring why they were there I was told, "There's no end of piracy in these waters, they're very necessary and armed to kill if we are boarded." Counting the hours off on the day we were due to anchor, Grandpa had a note from the Captain. It said, "Unable to anchor tonight, visibility nil, gales and blizzards make conditions impossible. Very sorry." I've still got it in my little box of treasures. So we waited and hoped. The seas were running so high we'd been at anchor for two hours before we realised it, as our vessel was still tossing about like a cork.

Still, we had arrived at last. Little did I know what a memorable time of our career was about to begin. Never will I forget my first sight of Wei-Hai-Wei and the little island of Liukungtao which was to be our home for the next three years. Everything but everything was snow white. Even the few sampan men, tossing about in their boats around the Shenking, were covered with snow. Having dropped anchor at least three miles from the shore, a steamboat (later to be our own little craft) came out to take us to the land. Watching it trying to come alongside took my breath away. One moment it was up in the air above deck level, only to disappear a second later into a great trough, seemingly forever. How were we going to get the children onto that, never mind ourselves? In a trice, one of the Shenking's officers seized little Jocelyn and literally threw her across the gap into the waiting arms of a huge, burly Chinese coxswain. I thought she'd had it! But he'd chosen the critical moment when the steamboat was just "passing" where we were standing! Jill being bigger managed to make a successful unaided leap for it by herself as did Grandpa and I. A nightmare trip to the Iron Pier, as I later discovered it was called, was followed by a hair raising and painful disembarkation. The waves froze solid as they broke over the metal, and it was caked with ice. Jocelyn went flat on her face, the moment her feet landed on this deadly skating rink.

But, at long last, we'd made it. Cold, wet, and somewhat shaken up it's true, but most definitely we were actually there!

CHAPTER 8
Liukungtao

Residences, activities and events

Temporarily, we lived in the Officer's Mess, as our predecessors were still occupying what was to be our bungalow, whilst waiting to leave on the Shenking's return journey. To say we were well looked after is putting it very mildly. Utterly amazing was the arrival of dozens, and I mean dozens, of the most lovely gifts; sets of silver spoons, a fur coat, beautifully embroidered bedspreads and tableclothes, kimonos, etc. It looked like a spread of wedding presents. Gobbling away in the backyard were six live turkeys. A most elaborate box came containing five huge hams! The children were inundated with toys, games and all manner of novelties and thought they had dropped into paradise. And everything had come from people we had never set eyes on! There seemed to be no end to the retinue of smiling faces at the door bringing extravagant offerings. Unused to anything like this I asked the couple we were relieving, what it was all about, only to be assured that it was entirely customary. If I as much as hinted that I couldn't accept the gifts, I'd cause deep and lasting offence. When I saw what their own departing gifts were like I realised mine were really quite modest in comparison.

Our drawing room, behind the prominent bay
window, was often used in the afternoons by naval
officers taking tea. The childrens nursery is
obscured, to the right.

Two amahs looked after the children. The old amah is
seen here holding Peter and the young amah Paul,
two of our three dogs.

All of these presents came from local tradespeople in the hope and expectation of our future custom. Not just our personal custom but dockyard and club contracts — really big stuff. Accepting the presents with gratitude, I nevertheless felt just a bit guilty at the same time.

Liukungtao really was a little paradise, though it did have one or two snags about which we had already been warned. Like no running water or conventional sanitation. Being so small, a mere two and a half miles long and three quarters of a mile wide, we could hardly be surprised that the "loo" was just a "tub", a box of sand with a small shovel alongside! The first time Jill saw this she said, flatly, "I'm not going to use that!" "Yes, you are", I told her, "There's nothing else on the island, everyone else uses them." "Well, I'm not", was all she would say, going off in a sulk. We got used to it, and, as it was emptied twice a day, it was as sanitary as possible. This emptying process involved opening a trapdoor behind the seat. One memorable day whilst sat there myself, I suddenly felt a blast of cold air, the trapdoor being banged heavily several times. I leapt smartly to my feet hoping the coolie wouldn't know exactly who'd been sitting there — it was all very embarrassing!

The bathroom was unique. A huge boiler was kept going with live coals burning in a fire box quite open to view; very comforting indeed it was in midwinter. Bathing had to be done in one of those awful hip bath affairs in which one sat with knees tucked under the chin. All the bath water had to be brought in buckets from the only well a mile away at the far end of the island. Horrified that the previous occupants had been content with these arrangements, I agitated for a proper bath with an outlet pipe. Impossible I was told, but persisting, eventually getting my own way. An outlet channel was dug, although where all the water went to after it left us I'd no idea. This modernisation programme at least saved the servants from the chore of baling out the dirty water with buckets. Of course they still had to fill it that way.

Our milk supply was very suspect, coming in empty beer bottles with a screw of newspaper in the open top. It was always boiled but one day I had to draw Grandpa's attention to its extreme thinness. A sample was analysed at the hospital, where it was found to be 10% water and containing live mosquito larvae into the bargain! I expect the delivery fellow, having taken a swig, topped up the bottle from the village pond. Yenza, our No. 1 house boy — major domo, butler and Grandpa's valet — was instructed to speak very firmly to the coolie who brought the milk, warning him it would be tested every day. He was also given a special bottle to use. Besides Yenza the bungalow staff of eight had been there for many years, my cook and the No. 1 garden boy for thirty years, the No. 2 garden boy eighteen years, and so on. All were as perfect as anyone could dream of, I adored every single one. I thought at first they might be critical of new ways and different methods but no — they made me feel my ideas were even better than anything they had met with before. Cook (whom I'd been told might be a difficult customer) became devoted to me, and I to him. His English was so poor I had difficulty in ordering the provisions. He'd bring the proposed menu each morning and I'd order accordingly, but his mispronunciation of names completely perplexed me, so I began asking him to name things in Chinese. I quickly picked up enough Chinese to do all my ordering this way which clearly delighted him and endeared me to him forever. I'd been puzzled at all the "cut flowers" that kept appearing, as we had a garden full, until I discovered he was confusing the words with the cauliflowers I'd ordered. Daily, I enjoyed my wrestle with cooks English, with both of us ending in fits of laughter. His very dour and forbidding appearance belied his real cheerful character, and we got on like a house on fire. His display of gold teeth when he laughed fascinated me. I didn't find it funny though when he told he how his previous employer would scream at him or hurl the order book at his head. I wondered how he'd managed to have the patience to try and please this virago? I was yet to discover that infinite patience and tolerance are chief and most lovable characteristics of these wonderful people. The No. 1 boy was Yenza, a thin, six foot tall, very slightly stooping northern Chinese. Like all of them really, nothing was too much trouble for him. He would wake me every morning with a delicious cup of tea, so exactly as I liked it that I thought I'd never, never again in this life, ever be so happy again. And I was right.

I had to learn of their very different ways and ideas of course, as they lost face if anyone tried to ease their work in front of their friends. My rickshaw (no cars, only bicycles and rickshaws), was pulled by a dear smiling "boy" (man, really). "Stop", I'd call out, "I'm getting out at this hill." He'd protest but eventually let me have my way. Great hulks of chaps from the ships would sit blandly in their rickshaws, letting their poor little undersized, underweight Chinese pull them along, struggling up the steepest hills. I'd tell them off, saying things like, "Get out you lazy creatures," until one old hand informed me that by getting out myself and walking up the hill I was subjecting my little man

The No 1 gardener is seen carrying water in a watering can and also in two old tin drums. The water was needed not only for the garden but also to fill the bath!

More household staff. From left to right, Cook, Yenza's son, Old amah, Yenza our "butler cum valet" and Mio.

to a most fearful loss of face. His friends would taunt him that he wasn't strong or able to do the same work as them! That staggered me. Sorting out these strange Chinese attitudes and customs was just one of my many problems. I was told never to offer to do my own shopping for provisions. That was cook's prerogative and he got some "cumshaw" from making purchases on my behalf. If I did my own shopping it would look as if I was trying to do him out of this!

I so loved these gentle smiling people. Wherever we went we were met with smiles and greetings. Shy, bright eyed, rosy cheeked, runny nosed children would gather round the garden gate, hoping for sweets. I once lured them all into the garden to be photographed with Jocelyn all clutching their glass jars of boiled sweets. Where are they now? Whatever happened to them? I wonder. As I write these very words the crayonned portrait of my dear head gardener, who grew such gorgeous flowers and vegetables for us, looks down on me. The conventionally serious expression he adopted for this picture, has been beautifully captured by my artist friend Margery Fenton. She was brilliant at this sort of work and sold many of her pictures. We got to know her well, helping with her wedding arrangements. Jill and Jocelyn were bridesmaids at the wedding with both her and the groom being carried to the church in sedans, Chinese style.

Normally, unlike his picture, our No. 1 Gardener as we called him, always went about his work smiling. He had been doing our garden for thirty five years. I'd bought some packets of seed, I remember, and as I love gardening had decided to plant them myself. Busily scratching away I became conscious of a grinning figure standing behind me, watching. Feeling rather self conscious and unable with my poor Chinese to explain why I was doing his job, I just grinned back and handed him the seed packet, hoping he wasn't offended. Another time, whilst entertaining a large afternoon tea party, the drawing room door burst open and in rushed five year old Jocelyn excitedly dragging this dear soul by the hand, shouting, "Mummy, Mummy, you must look, it's a wonderful sight, gardener has got six toes on both feet!" I, and all the other guests, looked at his bare feet and, sure enough, he had! We were all greatly amused. No-one knew quite what to say, whether to congratulate him or what sort of remark would be appropriate. Although the dear soul looked pleased, I suspect he was very embarrassed and didn't know where to put himself!

All the Chinese on the island looked well fed and healthy in

Wei-Hai-Wai. Both Jill and Jocelyn were bridesmaids
at a stylish wedding when my artist friend Margery
married Michael Fenton. They went to the church in
sedans, Chinese style and are seen here leaving
under an archway of swords held by a naval guard of
honour made up of Michael's fellow officers.

sharp contrast to many poor souls elsewhere. It's very different
now, I'm happy to say, but in 1937 the stark poverty all about
made it a harrowing experience to go out into the streets of
Shanghai. Scab covered, ragged, filthy beggars clutched
desperately at one's coat. Faces half eaten away, some were
obviously suffering from smallpox. In those days, believe it or
not, there was no quarantine for smallpox, the poor wretches
suffering from it just walked about covered in scabs, jostling
with the crowds. Worst of all, tiny children, mere babies in arms,
would be carried by both women and men being so drugged
they looked more like wax dolls. A stick threaded through the
child's sleeves across its back, enabled the lifeless scrap to be
carried without it just slipping into a heap. They'd beg for
something for the dying child, and at first I was so appalled I'd
give whatever I'd got. But oh, what a mistake that was. For when

one got out a purse, beggars of all sizes and ages gathered round in a ring, all moaning for food, their outstretched arms and hands forming and impenetrable hedge. British ex patriots were advised never to give alms to anyone, as this always caused a large crowd of beggars to collect at once.

In Shanghai scenes and instances of utter deprivation and universal poverty abounded everywhere. Two such may serve to give an idea of just how bad conditions were for nearly all of the Chinese population. In a cafe one day I saw a lorry loaded with sacks of rice stop outside. One sack had split, the contents streaming onto the road. From nowhere ragged and emaciated women and men rushed up, falling to their knees and feverishly picking up this precious food grain by grain. This pitiful sight sickened me — I couldn't even finish my coffee, the price of which would have fed one of them well for a week. Rickshaw men queued up in a long line on the Bund waiting for customers to come ashore from the ships. In the bitter and icy winter gales and blizzards they sat there huddled in misery. At night, having nowhere to sleep, curling up in their rickshaws. Each morning the daily paper printed a list of the dead picked up from rickshaws and shop doorways. At Wei-Hai-Wei and on Liukungtao things were very different.

Shortly after arriving on Liukungtao, whilst exploring the island, we came upon a sort of tent with people milling about and putting large round white loaves on some stalls. All were dressed in white, with what looked like chef's hats on, so we took it for some sort of trades exhibition. In we went, only to hasten out again very apologetically when we found we were in the middle of a funeral party! The many exhibits were dominated by a large photograph of the deceased. Grinning faces and deep bows all about had misled us into thinking we were welcome, not realising these actions really showed their extreme embarrassment. Walking back home we passed through the little cemetery and looked at the graves. Not for long though, as many gruesome sights were lying about, bones that had been exposed either by dogs or the weather. The Chinese seem to bury their dead on top of the ground, only casually covering them with a small mound of earth.

Considering the island was so small it had a surprisingly large number of buildings but still remained a lovely place. Covered with Japanese fir trees only seven or eight feet high it had a lovely nine hole golf course. The fragrance of wild thyme filled the air as one walked along, crushing the herb's tiny leaves underfoot. All of us played golf there, even the children.

Two of the buildings were small wooden churches, more like village halls really, one being Roman Catholic and the other Church of England. The R.C. Church was only used when the Fleet came up in summer, bringing their own priest. The C. of E. establishment was used throughout the year, a missionary padre coming from the mainland to take a communion service every Sunday, the communion vessels being kept in our house. This missionary had breakfast and refreshments with us before and after the morning service. One day I answered his, "Shall we see you at the Communion next Sunday, Mrs. Pomfret?", more directly than usual by replying, "No, I can't come, I haven't been confirmed!" That did it. He almost rubbed his hands together whilst he responded, "Oh, I'll attend to that! I'll come over once a week to give you instruction and when the Bishop of Shantung comes down you can be confirmed." He did as he'd said and I was duly confirmed with one Chinese boy and a midshipman. For all the good it's done me they could have saved themselves the trouble. It all seemed to afford them great satisfaction, much to my amusement. Long ago I left the orthodox church with its dogma, creed and ritual, ceasing to wrestle with my conscience in an effort to believe the ecclesiastical fables that are represented as truth. After many years of deep thought and reading I now have a deep, satisfying and unshakeable personal belief and spiritual philosophy. I'm totally convinced that our entry into the next world has nothing whatsoever to do with any particular religion (or none at all for that matter). I have to smile when I think of the satisfaction this Padre gained over the few Chinese converts he managed to collect, as after the service, they went straight back home and burnt a joss stick — just in case!

Apart from our residence, the best house on the island was naturally reserved for the C-in-C Sir Percy Noble and his guests. Sir Percy and Lady Noble came up each year until World War II started in 1939. Charming people, we saw a lot of them. I always cherish a particular compliment he paid me in conversation elsewhere, that I heard about from another Naval wife. It seemed he had said he was very fond of the Pomfrets, Carlene Pomfret being one of those people who was always there when she was wanted, and never there when she wasn't. What a nice thing to say, I thought.

Every summer we would get all the other houses dotted about on the island ready for the many wives and families who had followed their husbands out from England. They came up to us every year to escape the summer heat of Hong Kong by staying on our cool island. In winter time there'd only be a cruiser and a destroyer anchored in the bay so we got to know the ships officers very well, exchanging hospitality with them being lots of fun. The officers from HMS Suffolk were all particular friends of ours, as Suffolk had made many trips to Wei-Hai-Wei. Returning from an afternoon stroll at tea time, we'd often find half a dozen or more of them waiting for us in the drawing room ready for some tea. Cook's potato scones and his orange cake were particular favourites. I used to get him to bake an extra cake for Commander Stranack to take back on board his ship. Knowing him well, I was deeply saddened to hear he had gone down with his ship during the war. These young officers gave us a lot of laughs. One day in my absence they had a go at a cellular blanket I was crocheting, making a fearful mess of it. Commander P.S. Smith vowed he was an expert at knitting and said he'd prove it. He kept his word, sending me a navy blue scarf he'd made with his own hands.

One year we asked some friends who were going to Shanghai just before Christmas on HMS Suffolk to do some Christmas shopping for us. The island shops were only good for things like materials, and we wanted toys, dolls and good books for the children. They went off on this short trip with a long list of what we wanted. A day or so before they were due back, Grandpa got a signal, "Prepare to accommodate eight cases of smallpox on arrival". Grandpa replied, "Suffolk request turn back. No accommodation here for smallpox cases. No sanitation or water". But it was too late and arrive they did. All our eagerly awaited Christmas presents had to be burnt for fear of infection; we never even saw them. Even Suffolk's own doctor caught the disease very badly. Our little Naval Hospital was swiftly turned into an isolation hospital. Grandpa attended to all patients five times a day with only one sick berth attendant to help him. Each time he came back home the children rushed to him as usual, driving me frantic with worry. We were all re-vaccinated with fresh vaccine from Shanghai, and my word, what scabs we got, the size of teaspoons! There was no doubt this must have been a particularly virulent variant of the smallpox "bug". The hospital itself was on our very doorstep, not more than thirty yards from our bungalow. Being on a hillside with the hospital below us, we could literally see into the wards just by standing at the edge of the garden lawn.

Things looked worse and worse with the smallpox cases, one poor young chap dying two days before Christmas. In places the snow was piled waist high and the ground was frozen absolutely rock solid, so it was impossible to dig a grave for some weeks.

Grandpa of course had the job of writing to the deceased's parents to break the awful news. Eventually the rest of them got better, although Suffolk's doctor and some of the others were dreadfully scarred. The relief we all felt when the outbreak was over and they had all finally gone was truly enormous.

Wei-Hai-Wei
Geography

Wei-Hai-Wei lies in Latitude 37.30' N and Longitude 122.10' E on the south side of the Gulf of Pechili near the easternmost point of Shantung Province. On the mainland the district has an area of about 260 square miles. About three miles away is the island of Liukungtao which is the "Wee-Eye" of the sailors' affectionate memory (see figure). The Bay of Wei-Hai-Wei forms an extensive deep-water harbour. With the island forming a natural breakwater, the anchorage is well protected except from the North-East. In the middle of the harbour is Sun Island with the ruins of an old fort. It is about 1,200 miles to Hong Kong and 480 to Shanghai.

The China Fleet in the 1930's

This consisted of the five ships of the Fifth Cruiser Squadron (surely these "County Class" cruisers were the most comfortable to live in that we ever had?). HMS *Medway* with her Submarine Flotilla. One aircraft carrier. One destroyer flotilla. One cruiser which spent 9 months of the year alongside at Hankow (600 miles up the Yangtse) only emerging for her annual holiday and Fleet exercises. During her absence, one of the sloops took over the guardships duties at Hankow. Three or four sloops. All these ships, except the river gunboats, spent most of the summer in Wei-Hai-Wei.

The general routine was that, at the end of April, the main Fleet left Hong Kong and sailed north to Wei-Hai-Wei. Here it remained, working and playing hard till October. Individual ships went on short flag-showing cruises to many different ports. The climate of Wei-Hai-Wei, both in winter and summer, was well-nigh perfect and I well remember the tingling feeling of positive health which one felt at all times there. The sloops tended to be on duty at the opposite end of the station to the Fleet. We had hot, sticky periods in Hong Kong and up the Yangtse and came north to the snow and ice in the winter.

During the winter months, the anchorage at Wei-Hai-Wei was almost deserted, but a sloop or a destroyer would drop in for a few weeks at a time. We tended to spend a good deal of time at Chinwangtao (190 miles to the north) where the English owned Kailan Coal Mining Administration had their headquarters. Here we could lie alongside, though lightly frozen in. From Chinwangtao it was an easy visit to the Great Wall of China, which ended at Shanhaikwan, so that some of the essential but indelicate rituals needed to qualify officially as an "old China-bird" could be performed.

Medical Arrangements

The appointment of Medical Officer in Charge, R.N. Sick Quarters, Wei-Hai-Wei, was held by a Surgeon Commander who was always a general surgeon. When the Fleet was absent he wore another hat, unique for a Medical Officer, that of Resident Naval Officer. When the Fleet arrived in April, a medical "mate" came up from HMS *Tamar*, backed by a full complement of Sick Berth Staff, and RNSQ was open for business. The climate was so good and the open-air life so healthy that the health of the Fleet was generally excellent. But if there was any mild epidemic, the Medical Officers and Sick Berth Staff from the Fleet backed up.

Sometimes an extra specialist was available. For example, in my time the PMO of HMS *Medway* was an ENT Specialist.

It will thus be seen that during the summer months the MOIC had an interesting life of full professional endeavour. But when the Fleet left in October he became the leisured laird of this wonderful little island, with golf, shooting and fishing all laid on. His winter solitude was shared by a Naval Store Officer (also married) and a Sick Berth Petty Officer. I had a feeling that almost every young Medical Officer said to himself, "Some day I *must* become MOIC, Wei-Hai-Wei!" (I know I did.)

The End of an Era
I am most grateful to Surgeon Rear Admiral A.A. Pomfret, CB, OBE, who was the last of the line of MOICs, for an account of the end of the story. He says, "The Japanese occupied Wei-Hai-Wei in March 1938. In general they respected the British concessions on Liukungtao but there were several incidents from time to time. Finally in 1940 they refused to recognise a renewal of further concessions. Everything of value, including the steamboats, was sent to Hong Kong without trouble and finally, I was withdrawn and proceeded to Shanghai and on to the UK in mid-1940. There was no hand-over and no interference with my departure. As regards the local inhabitants, several including Jelly-Belly, went to Hong Kong, many joined the guerillas on the mainland, but as far as I know I don't think that many were murdered by the Japanese."

The paragraph above, together with those before describing the China Fleet in the 1930's etc., are reprinted from an article in the Journal of the Royal Naval Medical Service, 1975 by Surgeon Captain Harald Curjel, for many years a friend and colleague of S.R.A. A.A. Pomfret.

CHAPTER 9

Liukungtao II

Dogs, cats, magpie, beach parties, much socialising. A magnificent cruise to the Great Wall of China

When we moved in to our bungalow the children were overjoyed to find that we'd inherited three little dogs. Jill particularly took to Paul, a white, long haired Maltese terrier, with extremely potent bad breath, probably due to his bad teeth. We couldn't do anything about this as there wasn't a vet on the island. Paul eventually got an obstruction and died in my arms on the way to the hospital. One of our dogs, Jamie, was actually a female, despite her name. A nervous brown Cairn, her vocation in life seemed to be having puppies, preferring mincing Paul's attentions, who never failed to oblige, to those of our third dog, Peter. A rare mixture of Peke and Pug, Jamie would snarl at Peter if he came within a yard of her, even though he'd beg, standing on hind legs by her basket, before coming to me for help. I wasn't much use I'm afraid, for I could only tell him, "It's no use old chap, you've no sex appeal so far as she's concerned." We had no difficulty in finding a home for all of Jamie's puppies, or indeed her when we had to leave, getting the nuns on the mainland mission to take her when we left. Poor Peter though, the least lovable of the three, also had to contend with dreadful eczema.

He'd had this since birth, and it irritated him so much that he'd crawl under the sofa and scratch himself until he bled. Treating the rash as best as I could with calamine lotion, I covered his raw back with gauze. In summer this awful rash distressed him greatly. I put him on a meat-free diet, giving him raw eggs instead. But he would scavenge for meat and once I was told, "I saw your 'one egg dog' down in the village today demolishing a cod's head." He was totally undemonstrative even to me who did everything for him, yet he was by far my favourite, and I loved him dearly. The week we were due to leave I took him on a final walk finishing up at the hospital, where they put him down with their last dose of chloroform. Afterwards, I cried for days. I had to do it though, for the Japanese were coming and I knew what they'd do to him. He would have been thrown out and probably killed, maybe by being run through with a sword.

All the dogs had their own baskets, but when the puppies arrived Jamie was very cunning. Getting a bit fed up with them after ten days or so, she'd sneak them into one of the empty baskets at bedtime. By the time Peter ambled innocently along, he'd find the only one available was filled with wriggling, yelping, hungry puppies. After studying the other two occupied baskets he would very reluctantly get in with the heaving riotous mass. Immediately they would set about him, chewing his ears, climbing on his back and trying to feed from him. Peter was wonderfully patient and sweet with the puppies, whilst Paul, their real father, would have nothing to do with them. Firmly I'd turf Jamie out to lie with her offspring so that Peter could have some peace in his own basket.

Bachelor Captain Coppinger of HMS Capetown was a frequent visitor always accompanied by his dog Tiny, ("China's No. 1 dog" as he called him), to whom he was devoted. Whenever he visited us I'd lock my possessive three on the verandah to avoid a probable confrontation, with what they regarded as an invader of their territory. Arriving unexpectedly with his master one day Tiny was set on by our three and a first class fight ensued. Feverishly Captain Coppinger hung on to Tiny's leash, thus getting himself right in the middle of this yelping tangle. Suddenly, he cried out, "I've been bitten", (my Peter got the blame). Sure enough, blood was pouring from the back of his leg. Many hands separated the dogs, whilst I cleansed and dressed the injuries with hot water, iodine and bandages. I don't think Peter intended to show aggression to a human; but we didn't get many visits from Tiny after that though! Out walking, Peter had a habit of charging any dog we met, with terrible threats and growls. If the oncoming dog looked like putting up a fight for it, Peter would swiftly retreat behind our legs to leave the other two, coming up behind to enter the fray even though they weren't at all eager for a fight.

My dislike for cats dates from the time when we had a very tame magpie. The children were always bringing in injured victims, mainly birds, to be nursed back to health. Although I had said, "Please, no more casualties if possible", they smuggled in a baby magpie one day. Indeed, it nearly hit me in the face as I went into the nursery! So young that it had to be hand fed, this bird became incredibly tame, lovable and totally unafraid of us and the dogs, even feeding with them from their dinner bowls. Indeed, eventually it so intimidated them that a tall bird table was made, her meat being put on it. This magpie would still fly down to see what they were having though, much to their dismay, and steal bits of their dinners. Always with us, even sitting on the breakfast table trying to sample everything, she once got her beak stuck in the butter and had to come to me to have a huge lump removed. Coming with us to the church on Sunday, so that she could stay with us, she'd disrupt the service, often perching on the sailor's shoulders. She'd fly about the trees in the garden appearing with a rush if one called "Maggie" to sit on one's head or shoulder. Whilst we were away on holiday the servants told us she became quite frantic, searching for us everywhere, creating great havoc with her screeching and clucking until our return, when her delight knew no bounds. When I called her in the mornings she would sit on my bed and peck at the pink nail varnish I always used in those days. I suppose she thought it must be something worth eating. After about a year, I heard a fearful commotion outside one morning. Investigating, I shrieked with horror when I saw five alley cats on the hospital roof tearing poor Maggie to pieces! The servants came running and between my sobs I told Yenza, "You see those cats? I want you to get every single one of them caught and killed." "Yes Missy", he replied. I never set eyes on them again. I expect they had been abandoned and just roamed the streets and gutters, breeding indiscriminately. But from that day I've had no use for cats.

I've often been asked how the children got any sort of education? For a time exercise and text books were obtained from Shanghai until one day, as I was battling with some mathematics, Jill pertly remarked to Jocelyn, "I don't believe she knows the answers any more than we do!" Absolutely correct of course. I felt the time had come to retire from the scene and find someone who knew what they were doing. Casting about me I discovered Mrs. Swales, a storekeeper's wife who had done some teaching and a trained nurse into the bargain. Childless herself, she jumped at the chance when we suggested she took them on, as it gave her something to do and some money as well. Two little desks were made and the required books, stationery and equipment obtained. We even put the girls into gym slips and white blouses so that they would feel it really was school and not just some sort of game. I feel sure they must have learnt something for when they eventually went to school in Bermuda, they didn't appear to be behind in their work for their age group besides fitting in well.

Mrs. Swales, came in very useful indeed for another event soon after we arrived. We'd become very friendly with Yvonne King and her husband, a young couple living on the mainland, where he was head of the Chinese Customs. Sally, their only daughter was the same age as Jocelyn, so they often came over and spent the day with us. Yvonne King, a sweet French girl who spoke perfect English, was expecting a second child. She seemed very worried when I enquired where she was going to have it, saying uncertainly, "Well, Shanghai, I suppose." With Shanghai a thousand miles south and the Chinese/Japanese situation worsening daily, this didn't seem a very good idea, and we expressed deep concern. We all knew how badly the Japanese were treating passengers on the Coastal Steamers. Besides other indignities, they were now lining them up on deck half naked for hours on end waiting for a doctor to come, when he was good and ready to examine them, demand specimens etc. Apart from this, it also meant going down there a month before the baby was due as coastal steamers only ran to an infrequent schedule. To avoid all of these problems our nursery was turned into a maternity ward, Grandpa delivering the baby and Mrs. Swales attending as a nurse afterwards. Regrettably, I lost touch with the Kings after 1945, only knowing that they eventually settled down somewhere in Australia.

We became great friends with the British Consul, Scott Burdett and his wife Eileen. A sweet, middle aged couple they'd been married for years when suddenly to their joy had their first child. About two when we arrived, they doted on him, openly regarding his arrival as a miracle, spoiling him terribly. The long running war between China and Japan was still going on of course. Sometimes Japanese planes would roar over us, so low that we could actually see their pilots, on their way to dive bomb the mainland. One day the children and I were sitting on the

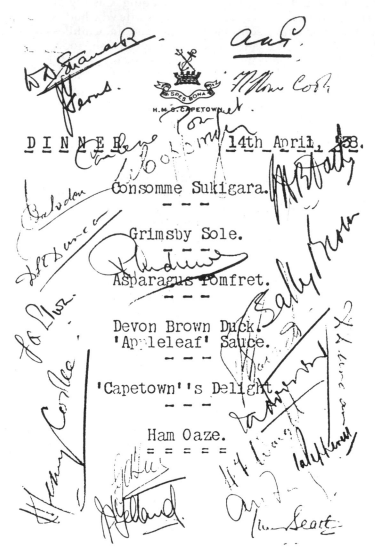

H.M.S. CAPETOWN

D I N N E R   14th April, 1938.

Consomme Sukigara.

- - -

Grimsby Sole.

- - -

Asparagus Pomfret.

- - -

Devon Brown Duck
'Appleleaf' Sauce.

- - -

'Capetown''s Delight.

- - -

Ham Oaze.

= = = =

We often dined aboard one of the ships moved off We-Hai-Wai. On this occasion we were entertained in the wardroom of the cruiser Capetown. The dishes on the menu above refer to vessels in the British Fleet, and a Japanese ship. One course is named after us! Most of the autographs are of friends and acquaintances I refer to in the text, and whom I remember with affection.

bungalow steps, watching one of these raids, tense with anxiety for our friends who lived over there. We were still safe, as our war was yet to begin. Suddenly, through our garden gate came a procession of people including a young Robert, the Consul's son and heir, his nanny, a cot, a pram, and several trunks. They had arrived to stay, explaining that a huge anti aircraft gun installed beside the Consulate was being used at intervals throughout both day and night, making a tremendous noise. Sleep was impossible, apart from the quite considerable danger. Most willingly we opened up our nursery for them to stay until things had quietened down a bit. Robert was a handful though. Defying me, he marched deliberately up and down my bed of daffodils just about to open. I dealt with him as I'd been longing to do for some time. I dare say his English Nanny had been told to go easy on chastisement. My two had amahs, who would never chastise a child of course, but they were never spoilt. Living the wonderful life they did, Jocelyn and Jill could so easily have become spoilt, but people who knew them as children have assured me they never showed any inkling of such a trait.

By good luck or by a good constitution I know not, but both of my children seemed to keep pretty fit wherever they were, apart from the occasional cold or tummy upset, surviving all the ups and downs very well. Jill, never at a loss in an emergency took rapid action when, unusually, both Jocelyn and her amah became suddenly ill whilst Grandpa and I were at a film show and dinner dance on board HMS Suffolk. Although only ten years old she phoned the signal station, saying, "Jill Pomfret speaking. Take a message to HMS Suffolk. Mummy please come home, Jocelyn and amah very sick." Grandpa got the message first, and dashed off at once.

Life was full of incident. I'll never forget one particular night when we had dinner on a destroyer, in the company of eight friends. I'm sure they won't forget it either, if they are still living. Ready to go home, the Commander told us very seriously that a signal had just arrived saying, "No liberty boats allowed to go ashore" and we couldn't possibly get ashore. Four miles out in the bay, the seas had whipped up far too much for safety. Groans of protest came from everyone, with general agreement that staying on board for the night was out of the question. After much debate, and getting many warnings, we set off in spite of this warning in an open Liberty Boat. The whole fleet had been told, so every ship had its searchlight trained on us. I've been frightened quite a few times in my life but this was truly horrific. Clinging to the sides of the lurching and tossing craft it seemed

"Tita". Jill captured this picture of
Tita showing off outside our
bungalow. In reality, Lady
Clark-Ker, the wife of the British
Ambassador, she never ceased
having fun in every way possible.
On this occasion she had rifled
Grandpa's wardrobe and is posing
outside the bungalow in his cap
and jacket above her own, for those
days, very brief shorts.

our end was near, with mountainous waves breaking right over us. I remember thinking, "Well, at least the sea is fairly warm, and if we finish up in it they surely won't let us drown." Up to our waists in water, we all lost our shoes and bags. Everybody was in the same plight, screaming, gasping for air and choking with sea water. Finally we reached the shore. I leapt for the steps but skidding on the slimy seaweed covered surface I slid down several, skinning both my knees. My lovely, tomato coloured, ankle length evening dress had shrunk to knee length, never to be worn again. The enquiry next day tried, unsuccessfully, to discover why a boat full of screaming women had come ashore, when the conditions had been declared unfit for any small boats to be launched at all. The men's uniforms suffered too, "Jelly Belly", the tailor, doing much trade the next day trying to restore them to at least wearable condition.

Early in 1939 the C-in-C signalled us to prepare a house for the Ambassador, his wife and their guests and servants who were coming up from Shanghai to stay for some months. Lady Clark Ker, or "Tita" as she became known to us, was a most beautiful and fascinating Chilian girl of twenty nine. Her husband, Sir Archibald, was nearly twice her age, and didn't stay long before going back, leaving the party to enjoy their holiday. The entourage included everyone Tita could collect together, her English butler, and his ten year old daughter. The girl's mother had been Tita's ladies maid, and had died in her service. I'm happy to say the child was wonderfully cared for and included in everything. And of course Tita's big liverspotted spaniel dog called Lupé came as well, so named after Lupé Valez the film star, a great friend of Tita's of whom she was inordinately fond. The group also included two teenage French girls, Monique and Miquette: their mother had been one of Tita's close friends but had died of leukaemia. A young couple, Jimmy and Bunga Barton, with their five year old son completed the party. We just loved everyone of them and it wasn't long before they all transferred themselves to our house.

Life soon became one long round of beach and tennis parties (we had three courts of our own). Tita was forever thinking up fresh ideas for outings and games and was thoroughly inexhaustable. She was a most gorgeous creature. All the men fell for her including Grandpa, of course. A platinum blonde (not by nature though) with huge, dark, sparkling eyes, fantastic black eyelashes, a brown skin and a beautiful figure. This she showed off to perfection, usually wearing the briefest of shorts. I have many photos of Tita and the parties she brought along. One

Wei-Hai-Wei. The Signal Station. Messages passed
between ship and shore through this station, by flag,
wireless, and semaphore. Jill once sent an urgent
message to me through this station when illness
struck whilst I was dining aboard a ship anchored in
the bay.

Wei-Hai-Wei. The Fire Engine. This historic machine
had many uses, including flooding the frozen pond
(shown above top right) to give a smooth skating
surface. Also used to pump out vessels at the
quayside it had to be manhandled to wherever it
might be needed.

shows her dressed in Grandpa's uniform and hat, with her brief shorts underneath, looking quite stunning. Another shows her dressed up for fun in Jill's clothes which fitted her perfectly although Jill was only eleven. I remember she upset the C-in-C one evening by appearing at a formal cocktail party on board dressed in her briefest of shorts. But of course he dared not tell the Ambassador's wife what she could or couldn't wear though. In any event Tita was a law unto herself. Bunga Barton (where she got the name from I've no idea) was a beauty too. An American Admiral's daughter she had below waist length luxuriant chestnut hair, worn quite loose except on formal occasions. Jimmy, her husband, a handsome, attractive man, had a Government job in Shanghai, so he didn't stay very long.

Ten miles out, about halfway to the mainland, was a tiny rocky speck called Sun island. Totally isolated and no more than three or four hundred yards across, it had nothing on it but rocks, but with lovely sandy beaches when the tide was out. Hearing about this island Tita suggested that all the women and girls got together for an all day picnic. Only females went, including me, Bunga, the French girls, the children and of course Tita herself. Taking packed baskets, the little steamboat took us out and left us there with instructions to return and collect us at 4.30 p.m. As soon as the boat had gone, off came all our clothes and we paddled, swam and lay on the rocks in the nude. Absolute bliss. It quietly amused me to see that Tita was determined to be an entire blonde for she was indeed blonde all over. After lunch we lay sunning ourselves on the rocks. Then voices were heard. Amazed and embarrassed we found we were surrounded by a group of Chinese men and women searching for shellfish among the rocks. The men gave us no more than a passing glance but the women were fascinated, forming a chattering, laughing group all around us. I sat up and clasped my knees. "What do we do now?", I asked. Tita sat up too, looked round and replied, "Nothing. What have we got that they haven't seen before?", and promptly lay down flat again, closing her eyes. Soon it became clear that the Chinese womens intense interest was centred on Bunga's beautiful hair. They gabbled and giggled, chattered to each other and went up to touch her hair cascading over her shoulders in a rich brown torrent. I suppose they were so used to seeing white women with short hair that they never realised that anyone other than themselves ever had long hair of such a rich chestnut, so no wonder they were so intrigued. We had a fantastic time throughout the whole of that summer of 1938.

Tita and her usual party, plus dog of course, returned again the following year. A tragedy which struck the Bartons marred 1939. We were all shattered to hear that fearful floods had struck Shanghai. Jimmy had waded back home from an evening out through the waist deep, foul and stinking water, and had picked up some deadly virus. With no antibiotics available, the infection took rapid hold, and he died within two days. Tita took charge of Bunga and her child putting them on a plane to America. Jimmy's death saddened everyone as he'd been with us, a healthy, lively person only a few days before. We never saw Tita again, as war broke out only a month or so later in September 1939. News got to us eventually to the effect that she had become entangled with an American in Hong Kong, her marriage to Archie ending in divorce. Years later I read in the newspapers though that she had remarried him, by now Lord Inverchaple, and had gone to England. Later still, I read she'd been involved

HMS Falmouth. Under the command of Cmdr Cecil Hardy this sloop was at the disposal of the C in C of the China Station, Sir Percy Noble. Most kindly he placed it in our hands for a holiday cruise in August 1939. Together with Jill and Jocelyn, Grandpa and I had a wonderful time visiting the Great Wall of China, Chingwangtao and Pehtaiho. Our servants didn't enjoy it quite as much though, suffering badly from sea-sickness!

in a fearful car crash, sustaining severe facial injuries needing extensive plastic surgery. For anyone a disaster, but for Tita sheer tragedy. If she's still alive she would be eighty two: that too would be a tragedy for her. She always seemed much too beautiful and full of life to even imagine old age in the days when I knew her.

The C-in-C came up to Wei-Hai-Wei just once more, in the July before war was declared in September, telling us, "Now you Pomfrets — you've never had a holiday since you came to the island so I'm lending you HMS Falmouth for a week, complete with Ship's company. You can take her wherever you wish, she's at your command!" We were staggered and, of course, overjoyed. He added, "You'll have your own quarters but dine with the Captain in the Mess. Take some of your servants with you, an Amah, Yenza and one of the others. Say when you can be ready and have a good week's holiday." We were thrilled and the servants delighted at the prospect. Working out where we would go, we decided to see the Great Wall of China, Pehtaiho, Chinwangtao and around that area. We had an absolutely fascinating and fantastic trip, buying loads of curios and treasures in Pehtaiho, all later to be lost in the war years. Grandpa and Commander Hardy went water skiing and we did lots of sight seeing. Our arrival in Pehtaiho was rather saddened by Grandpa being whipped off to certify the death of a young English schoolmaster who had died whilst bathing in the sea. Other than this we thoroughly enjoyed our break, but oh, dear, the poor servants we had brought with us we practically never saw. When Yenza brought us our morning tea he was a delicate pea green — if ever a Chinese could develop this hue. I asked him, "Where is Amah, Mio?" And he replied, "Oh, very sick, very sick, can't stand up." I felt sorry for them as I'm no sailor myself and they had been looking forward so much to the trip. I never saw people more glad to be home. Three days after our arrival back at the island war was declared, dramatically altering the whole course of all our lives.

CHAPTER 10

Liukungtao: The Final Months

Some more good times. French and Italian ships call on us. The British Fleet leaves. Japanese warships arrive. War looms. Scorpion hunts and other diversions

The notoriously fierce Wei-Hai-Wei winters were of the Korean pattern, with snow up to the window sills and sheet ice everywhere. Always, they began with absolutely predictable snowfalls on November 10th and another much more fearsome fall on December 17th. Both happened with unfailing regularity, never being even 24 hours out of schedule. The temperature dropped to an unbelievable depth, even the dogs drinking water froze solid in the closed-in and stove-heated verandah.

Despite these arctic conditions HMS Dorsetshire anchored in the bay for weeks on end providing us with wonderful company, friendship and unforgettable parties. The Captain, his wife and daughter Betty were special friends. Several naval wives came north by coastal steamer at this time to stay while Dorsetshire was with us. Braving the bitter weather we most willingly accepted invitations to dine on the cruiser. Lying half a mile out to sea the launch that took us out tossed us around like peas in a drum. Betty and Mrs. Barry, assembling at our house before we started off together on one particularly savage night asked me, "Why don't you do as we do and wear 'Long Johns' under your evening gown?", adding, "After all no-one can possibly see what's under an ankle length gown". "What a good idea", I replied, immediately finding a pair of Grandpa's to wear under my black velvet evening gown, hiding them completely. It was an absolutely frightful night. Undaunted, we fought our way through the blizzard to the ship. Gingerly mounting the innumerable ice clad steps we were piped aboard and greeted by smartly saluting young officers standing at attention, ready to assist us if need be. Suddenly a huge gust of wind whipped my skirt up to waist height. Clutching at it in desperate haste, I was too late, and all was revealed. To my intense humiliation the young officers just doubled up laughing. Afterwards I told Betty, "Its all very well for you two to join in, but you've got them on as well. No-one knows that, do they?" It was only me that must have supplied the material for some humourous tit-bits to be related in the mess.

The continual festivities including afternoon skating parties, after lunch at our bungalow, with tea and a superb assortment of most delicious eats cook laid on. The favourite was

Wei-Hai-Wai. Skating. In winter I enjoyed skating on the island's frozen over natural pond with many partners. Here I'm enjoying myself with Cmdr. Westmacott. The pond was surrounded by small Japanese fir trees which grew all over the island.

the wafer-thin hot potato cakes oozing with butter. These were
tremendously popular.

A French cruiser, the La Motte Picquet, visited us in the
summer of 1939, entertaining us lavishly. At dinner I found I was
expected to drink more wine than I wished. The Captain, sitting
next to me noted this and queried, "Madam doesn't care for her
wine?" "Oh yes", I protested, "But I only take very little I'm
afraid". He suggested that I might like Vichy water but I begged
him not to trouble. Being a hot night, we strolled on deck after
dinner chatting in the company of a Captain Leach. Along came
the wine steward with a drinks tray including a large glass of
sparkling Vichy water for me!! I had to take it, but after only one
sip commented, "Oh, good heavens, its revolting! Whatever
shall I do with it?" Captain Leach promptly replied, "Pour it over
the side". Over the rail it went into the dark depths beneath
producing a loud howl of protest! I'd emptied it squarely into the
Captain's launch lying alongside waiting to take us home.
Giggling, we quietly melted away into the wardroom. More than
six feet tall, Captain Leach was of distinguished appearance,
quietly spoken and most charming. His smooth relaxed dancing
made it a joy to be his partner. Taking command of the Battleship
Prince of Wales on the outbreak of hostilities, he perished with
most of the crew when his command was sunk. I was shattered to
hear this on the radio, our only source of news when the Fleet
had gone.

A mere couple of weeks before war was declared an Italian
cruiser the Bartolomeo Colleoni paid us a visit. The crew
fascinated all of us (except the men!) all the ladies falling under
their latin spell. First class hosts they entertained us superbly.
Still summertime, Hong Kong naval wives hadn't yet gone back.
The lively, romantic members of the crew of the Bartolomeo
Colleoni found the presence of these attractive, personable ladies
an extra bonus. One had to be constantly aware that they were
fast workers. One evening The Paymaster did his best to lure me
into his cabin ostensibly to see his collection of miniatures! Why
he imagined an English girl would be so naive as to fall for this
I've no idea; one didn't have to be very smart to see through his
little ploy! I suppose he thought it was worth a "try"!

We missed them a lot when they left rather suddenly. The
ship was soon fighting in the Mediterranean, and was the first
vessel to be sunk in the war. I was horrified. Our friends for but a
few mere weeks, giving us their hospitality, so soon they became
enemies, their vessel sunk and themselves killed. It was all so
quick; it was the men we'd actually known, there hadn't been

The Fleet at the Wei-Hai-Wei anchorage, Bay of Pecheli. A familiar view for us all, this photograph was taken from the golf course on Liukungtao. The mainland of Wai-Hai-Wai can be seen in the distance with the fleet at anchor in the bay between. Individual vessels are hard to identify, but include 3 funnel cruisers like the Dorsetshire, 2 funnel destroyers (the Delight etc.), and a flotilla of submarines led by the Rorqual. The roughly square area of buildings at right centre is the Chinese village. Most of the shops, the signal station and the iron pier etc. on the waterfront are obscured.

time to change the crew. I couldn't join in with the rejoicing voice on the radio that told us of the tragedy. Still, I had to accept they would have done the same to us.

Never having been interested in politics, the implications of what war would mean had never occurred to me. Our little island was on a ninety year lease from the Chinese, being used as a naval base for the British Fleet who needed it to escape from the heat of Hong Kong during the summer months. All the wives and children that had come out to be with their husbands and fathers used to come up from Hong Kong by Coastal Steamer. Some would rent bungalows for the summer, although the majority stayed in the hotel. We were always told in advance of who was coming, as it was one of our duties to arrange for bungalows to be cleaned, servants hired, and any other comforts attended to. All the main properties on the island, the club, hotel and dockyard etc., belonged to the British for the duration of the lease. This was due to run out very soon, towards the end of our commission. China and Japan being at war, as soon as these properties reverted to the Government of China, the Japs were waiting to step in and take the lot! This made for a very tricky situation indeed. No one could possibly have handled it better than Grandpa!

Suddenly the whole Fleet, including HMS Falmouth just disappeared overnight and we wére left high and dry all to ourselves. Mr. Millard, the engineer, Mr. Shaddick, the chief shipright, and one sick berth attendant, were the only Europeans left on the island except ourselves. Grandpa had been told to remain where he was. There was nothing else we could do anyway. Imagine our astonishment then, when one morning we woke up to find the bay complete with the Fleet again. Then astonishment turned to annoyance as we realised that it was the Japanese Fleet, complete with its own Flagship, anchored in the very same berths our own vessels had so recently vacated. Japan was not yet at war with us, but they made it clear where their sympathies lay — definitely not pro British. Having decided that as they were already at war with China, anything belonging to the Chinese was theirs for the taking, they had arrived to take possession of the island. The British leases though, like our house, the signal station etc. they couldn't touch. Flying Union Jacks from our flagpoles gave us some sense of security, probably quite falsely. The Japanese landed one night and removed our flags. This caused no end of a row and after loud and angry protests the flags were replaced.

As Grandpa was in complete charge, he was fully responsible for all that went on and his problems increased daily, or more accurately, hourly, One he had to solve concerned our Chinese prison, full of all kinds of criminals from murderers downwards. The warders had all fled in sampans to join the mainland guerillas on hearing a rumour that the Japs were on their way, and were expected the next day. Quickly getting hold of the keys, with a little help he unlocked all the cells, giving each inmate a couple of dollars telling each man, "Be off with you as soon as you can." They needed no second telling. For one night at least, until they could get some form of transport, the island must have been overrun with criminals. I'm sure we were in no danger though, as they were all too concerned with saving their own skins to stop and do us any harm.

Our biggest worry was seeing the Chinese openly persecuted and being unable to hit back on their behalf. Naturally the Chinese were very distressed and apprenhensive about so many Japanese on the island. There were lots of nasty incidents. The Chinese couldn't understand why we were power less to protect them; our position was very dicey indeed.

Although diplomacy required the Japanese Officers to call on Grandpa and for him to return such calls, it must have seemed that we were fraternising with the Japanese in spite of their cruelties to the Chinese. Nothing could have been further from the truth, the Japanese were going out of their way to aggravate us as much as they could. One particularly foul way was to pick on any Chinese employed by the British. This realy got us steamed up, the more so because we were powerless to do anything about it, although Grandpa intervened as much and as often as he dared.

Soon it became very obvious that the Japanese were trying to intimidate us, but couldn't go too far, as war hadn't been declared yet. That was lucky for us, but we still had to take quite a few insults all the same. Groups of Japanese sailors would stand idly by leaning up against our gates and peering into the garden and house, with the children running in to tell me, "Mummy, Mummy, the garden is full of Jap sailors stealing our figs!" I used to fly out brandishing a black umbrella, yelling rude things at them making them flee like a lot of naughty school boys. In quiet moments I often wondered what I'd have done if they hadn't run off. Our confidence in the Union Jack was really quite pathetic. Little did we know that later on it would mean less than nothing to them. Our quiet little beach, where we picknicked, was invaded by groups of insolent Jap soldiers. Coming as near as possible to where the children and I were sitting, they would spit and urinate in front of us, giggling when we leapt to our feet, gathered up our belongings and turned for home. Even then I remember it never occurred to us to be frightened of them, only utterly contemptuous.

The Japanese Captain came to call on Grandpa at the house complete with a troop of fully armed body guards. When he was invited in, this gang tried to follow on behind. "Stop!", said Grandpa, "I'm not having that lot in my drawing room!", making them wait outside the front door. When the children and I came back from playing golf we found this lot sitting on the steps. Whatever was going on, we wondered. Later, when I found out, I told Grandpa, "You've got a nerve, they were a fearsome bunch and might have turned nasty." When Grandpa dutifully returned this visit going on board the flagship, he was offered raw fish and saki to eat and drink.

Dozens of irritating and humiliating incidents occurred and as time went by we began to get more and more nettled by the impudence of the Japanese, who it seemed just wanted to get rid of us any way they could. It vexed me to find Japanese sailors running alongside our rickshaws chattering at us for although I've no idea what they were saying I'm sure it was something insulting. They would throw stones at the dogs and generally make a nuisance of themselves. Yet it seemed very odd when meeting a group of them when we were out walking to find they had obviously raided some gardens with each man carrying a little posy of flowers in his hands. This seemed so out of character with the atrocities they could perform. One day whilst we were having lunch, three loud shots went off. I asked Yenza, "What on earth was that?" Looking downcast all he said, very quietly, was, "Better not ask Missy". I couldn't rest until I found out. Apparently the Japanese had caught some guerillas on the mainland, put them in a boat with some spades, brought them to the island beach and made them dig their own graves before shooting them and burying them on the spot.

All the time I was out on Wei-Hei-Wai I only went into the kitchen three times. Once was to tell cook that a new stove would be coming, as the old one was giving trouble. He greeted this news with horror, entreating me to let him keep his old one. Looking at the battered wood and charcoal stove, thirty years old at least, for the first time, and knowing his cooking just couldn't be equalled, I asked him, astonished, "Do you mean to say you've cooked all our wonderful dinners on that old thing?" Enthusiastically he replied, "Yes, Yes, Missy. No want any other please." So I gave in and got the blacksmith to come up and mend the old one instead, so, to his joy, he kept his old stove.

Another time during the Japanese occupation I went to the kitchen for something, and found it full of guerillas from the mainland! I was horrified in spite of the fact that they had brought us about six brace of pheasant! Having guerillas in my kitchen had me really worried. I told Yenza, "For goodness sake get rid of them, if the Japanese ever discover we've had guerillas on premises they'll shoot us and you too." The pheasant were most welcome though. In the months to come we got so sick of them we never wanted to see another. Meat had become in very short supply as the coastal steamers didn't come very often now. We got lamb from Cheefoo when and if we could but gradually it all stopped. The Japs probably pinched it all. I found out that Grandpa had given the guerillas all sorts of medical supplies, bandages, etc., and they were very grateful. When we were out playing golf, the Japs took the opportunity to walk into our house, look round, with the poor servants quivering with fright not daring to stop them. They showed particular interest in our radio set, convinced it could transmit as well as receive and that

"Showing the Flag". When the Japanese started to take
over Liukungtao, Grandpa decided to literally "show
the flag". He draped a large Union Jack outside the
Administrative Block, and prepared to "repel
boarders"!

we were up to no good. British news came through from time to
time, and we even heard about ourselves being the only family
on Wei-Hai-Wei, over-run with Japanese, and in a serious
position. They even gave out our names and ages (and getting
mine wrong!), where we came from and so on. It was rather a
thrill. For a full year and two months we lived our life on the
island wondering what would happen to us next.

Grandpa asked the Japanese Commander what would
happen to him if England went to war, to be told he would be
shot and his wife and family interned in a Shanghai camp. So I
can assure you we watched and listened to the war news with
great attention. We took each day as it came, going on walks,
playing golf (on still British property). It incensed us to see a
Japanese party going round it one day without even asking
permission. Grandpa was furious, and got this stopped
immediately. Its no wonder they looked forward to shooting
him! We no longer had dinner parties but now and again had
pleasant days when friends came over from the mainland to see
us. The formalities for them to do even that were most
aggravating, having to submit to being searched by these Jap
thugs, both on arrival at the jetty and when they left.

Looking back on the whole period now, though, I go cold
with horror, knowing of the unspeakable acts they committed in

the prison camps down south when war actually started. We were so near to getting the same treatment.

I'm choked with nostalgia for all those far off days as I look through my photo albums, press cuttings and books. One book, "The Life of a Fly" by Fabre has a handwritten message inside, "To Mrs. Pomfret, in memory of those happy scorpion hunts. From James Corbin". Whereby hangs a tale.

All my life I've been deeply interested in insects, finding a surprisingly varied collection on the island many of which I found unfamiliar. Cicadas, that nearly drove one mad in the heat of the summer, praying mantis of huge proportions and of course, scorpions. I'd read how female praying mantis ate their partners after mating, one day actually seeing this happen in a hillside hedge I was watching, the larger female quite casually and methodically devouring her beau from the head downwards, even before mating was completed. In autumn the females laid their eggs in a large blob of green froth that issued from them along with eggs deposited in rows till eventually it looked like a big green marshmallow sweet. In twenty four hours it set as hard as concrete. Only then did I discover that those odd looking lumps that I had been trying unsuccessfully to knock off walls and gateposts were praying mantis nests. These mounds of air bubbles insulate the eggs from the intense cold during the most severe of winters. I once read that this was how the idea of a thermos flask evolved. In the spring I used to watch all the babies hatch out in the warm sunshine.

Scorpions are quite another matter. I declared war on these horrors after I found one crawling up the inside of Jocelyn's mosquito net. A Naval Officer's wife was stung on the big toe when walking home at night from a dance. She had a fit of hysterics because she was under the impression the sting was fatal. It can be fatal to a child, and if not treated it can make a very nasty mess of an adult too. A frantic phone call fetched Grandpa and he was able to calm her fears, but it was still extremely nasty. I was always afraid that, as we padded about the bedroom floor barefoot, we might accidently tread on one of those brutes. Well, I decided that I would try to exterminate as many of them as possible. I used to go out at night with a torch and find dozens of them scuttling along with their supper held high in one claw. I'd knock their still alive supper out of the claw and then stamp on them. Mentioning this one night to one of my guests at dinner, I found that quite a few of them had never seen a scorpion so I asked them if they would like to partake of a scorpion hunt. They all said they would, so I got loads of torches, gave each couple one and sent them off in pairs to the most likely places. I heard many squeals of, "Oh, I've got one" followed by a thump. It was a highly entertaining and profitable pastime. We must have despatched an awful lot of them that night.

No such hunt could take place after the Japanese arrived, for, if they had seen us creeping around at night with torches, they would have been certain we were up to no good and come to investigate at the very least. One keen entomologist we knew was on his hands and knees on the railway line in Shanghai looking for a certain kind of ant with a magnifying glass. The Japanese didn't bother to enquire what he was doing, they just shot him in the bottom and he was in hospital for weeks.

The whole of 1940 was full of incident with signals flying to and fro all over the place. The Japanese gave Grandpa an ultimatum. "Go", they said. Grandpa replied, "I take my orders from the British Admiralty, not from you." Grandpa signalled the Admiralty, "What do I do?". Came the answer, "Stay where you are."

The Japanese infestation of the island made life very difficult indeed. Press cuttings we saw later said the situation was "very ugly". But still we stayed on. They tapped our telephone and listened in to all calls to the mainland, innocent though they were. As the year drew to its close it was obvious we would have to go, but how? No ships were calling at all now, and this was pointed out to the impatient Japanese. We had friends on the mainland, hotel keepers and one or two retired Government officials. They too expected the order of the boot. One very dear friend of mine, Elsie Clark, felt certain they would not be turned out as they held no official position. Her husband Ernest was a total invalid, the tragic result of a series of strokes. A complete wreck, unable to speak or feed himself, he relied completely on his two houseboys to do everything for him. Helpless as a newborn baby, he would just sit and smile pathetically, having to be fed with a teaspoon. Elsie was a very sprightly, go ahead, game for anything, type of person, coming over to spend a day with us every week. We returned these visits going to their most glorious bungalow full of utterly gorgeous treasures including priceless china and figurines. Elsie suggested the children and I stayed with her, should Grandpa leave before us, until the time came when we knew what our fate was to be. We considered the idea, but only briefly, for we didn't share her optimism. Without much thought we decided to get on the first ship possible away from the island, even if it only took us down as far as Shanghai.

The last three weeks of our stay on the island were very tense indeed. Grandpa sabotaged everything he could, rather than let it fall into Jap hands. One sleepless night he spent sorting through all the official papers with Mr. Shao, his delightful secretary and clerk, amidst much murmured conversation. Then they left the house together and were gone for the rest of the night. Later I discovered their clandestine activities involved taking all the confidential documents and lowering them down the deepest well they could find. (I expect they are there yet!).

We began to feel very nervous for every night, after we had gone to bed, we sensed the garden was full of Japs, who always went around fully armed. So, leaving Grandpa on the island for another three weeks, the children and I accepted Elsie Clark's invitation to stay with her on the mainland until we could get passage in a ship. At last the "Shuntien" made its last call and we hastily got ourselves on board. Our mountains of cabin trunks and packing cases full of our treasures had to be left behind in the Mainland Hotel never to be seen again. Of course we were very fortunate to get away at all. It was a most harrowing farewell, with the children and I and both amahs all at the end of the pier crying our eyes out. Had I known of their ultimate fate I can't imagine how we would have felt.

CHAPTER 11

Across the World Once More

*From Shanghai, across the Pacific and
Canada, finally arriving in Bermuda*

Reaching Shanghai after an uneventful trip, we went to the
Palace Hotel, the same one we'd stayed out on our way out.

Keeping in contact with the people we had left behind was
quite impossible. All the spasmodic letters we received had been
heavily censored by the Japanese, who cut huge slices out of
every page. So it was only much later that we found out about all
the terrible events that had gone on, making us very sad indeed.
When war was finally declared the Japanese set upon all the
remaining British residents and many Chinese as well. They
flung poor old Ernest Clark, the total invalid, into an open lorry
in the depth of the intense winter, afterwards going round
picking up just about anyone they could lay their hands on. Not
surprisingly, he died from this callous treatment. The Kings,
their two children (one born in our nursery) and Elsie Clark
finished up in Shanghai concentration camps. Elsie died there of
cancer, but the Kings, separated from each other in different
camps, managed to survive. Years later, a Chinese drinks waiter
at a cocktail party on a cruiser in Plymouth, gave us more news,
knowing Wei-Hai-Wai very well. I was shattered and horrified

to hear that Yenza, of fond memory, had been taken to the end of the iron pier and beheaded. So too was "Jelly Belly" the tailor (the name was even written up over his shop). Just because they had worked for the British. What barbarians the Japanese were.

Life went on as usual at the Palace, the food and attendance being excellent, although the building was surrounded by big, barbed wire barriers. Many diplomatic families we knew and had given hospitality to in Wei-Hai-Wei visited us, sometimes taking the children out for the day to their homes. Our rooms were on the seventh floor. One day, during a childrens party I gave, someone emptied the water from a large vase of flowers out of the window into the street below. The first I knew of it was when an irate manager appeared complaining that a very cross Chinese gentleman had been drenched. Much later I was told who was responsible and was relieved to find out that it wasn't one of my two. The weather was absolutely dreadful, snow and sheet ice covering the roads. Grandpa had a near miss out shopping one day, returning shaking and white as a sheet. He'd fallen flat on his face in the path of a double decker bus, being quite terrified when it only just managed to skid to a stop inches from his face.

Shanghai was our home for six weeks whilst we awaited the arrival of the "Empress of Britain", to take us away to Canada. Eventually, all packed and ready to go, the awful news came through that this liner had been sunk. We were in a real dilemma, for ships were now few and far between. All we could do was to change our money back into Chinese dollars and wait. Later we learned the "Empress of Asia" would be coming for us, providing that she too didn't get sunk on the way.

So we were obliged to stay on for another month. Although anxious to get away, I found staying on no hardship at all. We made some very congenial friends, going to as many night clubs and cabarets as we could find, in a group of six. We found plenty of all-night shows and gambling casinos, the quality of entertainment being first class. One evening I decided to take a look at the casino area. Putting a few dollars on the roulette wheel I came away all of twenty five dollars richer! In those days the Shanghai dollar was only worth one shilling and six pence (8p now), a very favourable rate of exchange. Consequently we bought all sorts of things to take with us. Grandpa even bought me a most expensive present. He took me to a shop that sold furs and I picked out a number of leopard skins. These were then made up into a beautiful coat and matching hat. One day I felt dreadful. Realising I was developing a frightful cold, I went to bed with all the appropriate remedies. Due to go out again with our friends, to some night spot or other, I felt too ill to join them, but Grandpa saw no reason why he shouldn't go. Not that I minded, but I felt more than a bit peeved when I woke next morning and saw his bed hadn't been slept in. He eventually turned up around breakfast time, but I wasn't much interested in the story of all the good times they'd had whilst I lay in my room alone feeling wretched!

There was dancing every evening in the hotel, in a delightful ballroom with an excellent band. We used to sit round the edge at small tables with our drinks and watch or dance as the inclination took us. One evening, sitting chatting, the very elegant debonair Russian Maître d'Hotel came up to us, making a stiff bow to Grandpa. In his best English he addressed Grandpa, "Monsieur, pardon, but may I ask your permission to dance with Madame". This came as a bolt out of the blue to me, as I'd never seen him on the dance floor. Naturally, as a rule the staff didn't join in social activities with the visitors. He was a most distinguished looking aristocratic type, but I'd no idea what he'd be like as a dancing partner. But I knew soon enough, for the moment we got onto the floor I found that here was an expert. He quickly recognised the fact that so was I, and we enjoyed a most unforgettable experience together. In halting English he told me he'd been a professional dancer, which didn't surprise me at all. I can't find the words to describe how absolutely wonderful and oh, so rare, it was to find someone of his calibre. So enthralled was I that I didn't notice the floor clearing completely. All the dancers were now onlookers, and we had the floor to ourselves in an exhibition number! Why Grandpa agreed so generously to the Russian's request I've no idea, as the temperature always used to drop the moment Grandpa so much as saw a man just heading my way! I wore a gorgeous evening frock that night made of tomato coloured brocade. In a Chinese style it had a high neck and long sleeves, very fitting to the figure, with frog buttons all the way down to the ground. My matching slippers had been specially made from the identical material, open toed with very high heels. Recalling this now from Xmas 1940, I wonder, in 1991, if the person writing it all down can possibly be the same person, now aged 83½.

Quite suddenly, without any warning at all, the Empress of Asia arrived in port. During that chaotic morning, we somehow managed to get packed and on board, the liner sailing at once for Victoria Island, Canada.

A beautiful ship, the Empress of Asia took us across the

Pacific to the continent of North America. As usual, I spent the first five days flat on my back in our cabin hoping to die. One or two of the more hearty passengers came to see me, making the usual comments and keeping me up to date with any pieces of news, which at that stage didn't interest me one bit! Marjorie Ham, a very nice and cheery naval officers wife was one of my visitors I remember. With the addition of a very charming and good looking young naval lieutenant, Marjorie made up a table of six with us in the dining salon. The first day I made it to the dining room, Marjorie greeted me with, "Oh, I didn't recognise you standing up, after only ever having seen you lying flat on your back in a bunk". We became a very close little "six-some", all of us having one thing in common — none of us knew what the future had in store for us. It's just as well we didn't know, for our charming young lieutenant was to be killed within a few months, and we ourselves were in for many trials and tribulations. The few weeks we had on board were to be our last bit of enjoyment for some time. One week was rather unusual, for we crossed the date line from west to east and so that week had eight days with two Thursdays, which puzzled me a lot! Of course, as on all voyages, the clocks had to be altered every day, so we never really knew what time it was anyway. Arriving at Victoria Island, in the flurry of packing, I quite missed breakfast, not even getting a cup of tea, having to settle for a cup of coffee. This looked and tasted a week old at least. I think it was too, for it pretty much took the lining off my stomach, or so it seemed, and I was quite ill for the next fortnight.

A short train ride took us into Vancouver where we had just enough time to enjoy a lovely day going round the City. I was rather frightened though as this was the first time I'd met cars driving on the right hand side of the road. The same day we embarked on what was to be an enthralling train journey through the Rockies and across the continent to Montreal. From there it was intended that we go on to St. Johns, New Brunswick, and get visas to go on to England. The train journey was spoilt for me though by what I really thought was a stomach ulcer for I couldn't tolerate food at all. I managed to enjoy the trip all the same, for it was certainly an experience of a lifetime, with magnificent scenery almost beyond description. I had a superb view of lakes, forests and snow-covered mountains through the window of our luxurious compartment. I'd commandeered the bottom bunk to be sure of missing nothing and gasped in wonder at the moonlight scene, going sleepless for most of every night, watching the spectacle rolling past. I even saw some moose! Places with romantic and fascinating names like Kicking Horse Canyon, Medicine Hat, and the Great Divide, marched past.

Not knowing how much money we'd need, we had to be very careful with our money, having to pay for each meal as we had it. Grandpa had worked out, that we could have a good breakfast, miss lunch and finish the day with dinner. Some other Naval Officers on the train would greet us each morning with, "Hello, Pomfrets, you'd better eat all you can, nothing more for you till tonight." Sometimes, at midday the train would stop at a little station with not much more than a tiny wooden platform and a food kiosk. They only seemed to sell apple pie and cheese which Grandpa would leap out and buy to augment our other meals. Eventually we rebelled, saying we never wanted to see any more of this fare for as long as we lived, particularly me still suffering from this miserable tummy.

We were locked in our compartments for the few hours our route lay on American soil, the attendant explaining that the authorities would intern us otherwise when we stopped, briefly, on their territory. I didn't quite follow why, as the Pearl Harbour attack was yet to happen and America wasn't involved in the war at all. Still, nobody came to inspect our compartment or the adjoining one the children were using. We spent the time looking at the panorama outside, with waist high snow piled everywhere.

For years to come the sound of a steam train with its moaning whistle would always take me straight back to that most unforgettable trip.

At Winnipeg we could get out and stretch our legs at last. About three steps though were more than enough for me — I couldn't get back into the train fast enough. The cold was beyond description. One's breath froze, one's nostrils stuck together and when I grasped the train door handle my gloves stuck to it instantly and had to be prised off.

Arriving at Montreal we were shattered to find there was no room for us at our hotel at all. Refugees from England and Naval Officers who'd arrived fresh from directing convoys and so on had filled every available room. The owner gave us coffee and discussed what could be done, finally offering us the room he used himself with his charming wife. The children had made up beds in our room as there was nowhere else for them at all. Playing in the corridor next day Jill and Jocelyn were accosted by a Naval Officer staying in a nearby room, who said, "Aren't you the little Pomfret girls?", and they acknowledged that they were.

I poked my head out to find out who they were talking to, to see an acquaintance we had made, and who had entertained us for the day in Columbo on our way to China. He became a dear friend whom we saw a lot of later on in our travels, even asking him to be John's godfather when he arrived in 1950.

Whilst at the hotel, we were hailed across the dining room by a Naval Convoy Escort Officer we knew. Coming over to us he asked, "What are you doing here?" On being told we were waiting for transport to England he exploded! "You're never thinking of taking those children into England at a time like this, are you? It's criminal! We're trying to get children *OUT* of England as fast as we can and you're actually thinking of taking them *IN*! You must be mad!" etc. etc. "Well", I asked, "Where else can we go? We can't stay here. Our Canadian dollars are fast running out, we can't get any more, we don't know anyone who might finance us, so what alternative is there?". "What's wrong with taking them to Bermuda?", he suggested. This line of thought hadn't occurred to us at all, and we decided to give the idea some thought.

Although the Canadian authorities had returned our passports, they refused to give permission for the children to travel to England. Our money was disappearing at an alarming rate. We'd never met this custom of paying and tipping at each meal, whilst resident in the hotel. Waiters sometimes didn't get a tip at all, for even though they might think us mean, we just didn't have the money. At one mealtime I was most embarrassed. Jocelyn had noticed an extravagant-looking dessert on someone's plate and said, "Mummy, I should like some of that". Swifly, Jill cut in with a penetrating, "Don't be silly, Jocelyn, that's on the dollar fifty side of the menu, we have what's on the seventy five cents page!" Pitying looks came from all over the room.

The idea of going to Bermuda was getting increasingly attractive. We discovered that the Twiggs, friends from South African days, were there, Surgeon Captain Twigg being in charge of the Royal Naval Hospital. Mrs. Twigg, who you'll recall used to try and train me in the niceties of convention, had been very ill with cancer, a condition she'd always dreaded. They replied to our cable saying they'd be happy to put us up temporarily, until we found some more permanent housing.

So, we decided to go. First, off we went to St. John's, there to await passage to Bermuda itself. Ship movements were kept secret until twenty four hours before sailing. Knowing we would have an indefinite wait, constantly at the ready, some temporary shelter was sought. First we went to an address that someone or other had given us. This was most unsatisfactory, a sort of pub-cum-guest house, tatty and depressing. Jill summed it up saying disdainfully, "Surely we are not going to stay here?" "You're right", I replied, "Not if I can help it." The landlord chatted us up until Grandpa finished attending to the luggage, whilst I felt progressively more and more uncomfortable, sure we would be walking out of the place very soon.

When Grandpa arrived he too decided it was awful. Never one to mince his words, he told the proprietor very bluntly that it wasn't suitable. Leaving, another taxi ride took us to an address on the other side of the town. This time we were luckier and though far from luxurious it was at least adequately clean. Getting a very pleasant welcome, it still felt very odd having our bedrooms on the first floor and then coming straight down into a restaurant, something I'd not met with before.

We'd had several introductions to Canadian families and they couldn't have been sweeter to us. One family in particular begged us to let the children stay behind with them for the duration of the war. A most generous gesture, but not one we could consider of course. By now it was January and the weather very fierce with snow everywhere. Thankfully we were well prepared and I'd got plenty of furs. One brown fur I'd been given had been made into a coat and hood for Jocelyn before we left Montreal. From the back she looked just like a little Teddy Bear. A huge Alsatian dog certainly thought she looked real enough. Leaping on her from behind with a terrible snarl he dashed the terrified child to the ground as we stepped out onto the street. Horrified passers-by helped us get the dog off her. Fortunately she wasn't hurt but I'm sure she remembers the incident very well.

Six weeks or more passed by in St. Johns, before a ship arrived to take us to Bermuda to be greeted very warmly by our friends the Twiggs. Three times in our career we shared their lives and got to know them well. Surgeon Captain Twigg was twelve years older than Grandpa and had been his senior officer several times. Poor Ivy Twigg was only to live two more years, dying in 1943, but was well looked after by a treasured maid they'd brought with them from England. She was cook, housekeeper and parlour maid all in one. A very sensible, rather dour looking person in her thirties but quite invaluable. So much so that when Ivy Twigg died, Frank Twigg married her. After Bermuda we never came across them again. Much to our surprise I heard that they produced a son when he was in his sixties, and an Admiral, retired.

CHAPTER 12

Bermuda

A bungalow of our own in a cedar wood.
New friends, new experiences, glorious
times

As soon as we could, we went over to Hamilton, the Island's capital, looking for a good agent to find us a house. We found an excellent agent, who eventually became a very close friend, in Jean Cookson, a most delightful person, attractive, vivacious, lively and great fun to be with. Remarkable in every way for not only was she a cute business woman, but in addition rode a bicycle, swam, played tennis, and looked after her husband despite only having one arm. The other arm had been severed in a train crash many years before, but her beautifully cut clothes concealed the fact so well that I never even noticed its absence as she took down particulars of what we required. Some of her garments had little capes which disguised her shoulder very well indeed.

Not able to remain in Bermuda for more than a week having to report to the Admiralty in London, Grandpa was off as soon as we had moved into a nice bungalow in Paget. His trip in a ship travelling in convoy with many others via New York was quite awful. Halfway to England both the ships ahead and astern of his in the line were torpedoed at the same time both exploding and being literally blown out of the water. It was a most horrific thing, as in convoys no one was allowed to stop to rescue the survivors as it put the rest of the convoy in immediate danger. Whilst he endured this terror, we were settling down to our new life in Bermuda, meeting a lot of other families in the same position as us. We felt a little bit guilty at our life style compared with that which our relatives and friends back home were having to put up with. Jean Cookson also found us an absolute treasure of a maid, a dear girl, black as coal girl, called Ismay, a most

106

Jean Cookson. A lively and entertaining businesswoman, who helped to find us both of our homes on Bermuda, and in many other ways. Seen here taking tea in the garden of her own bungalow, she had overcome the drawback of only having one arm, riding a bicycle, playing tennis etc. She was adept at disguising the absence of her left arm, wearing caped jackets, for example, as in this photograph.

sophisticated, attractive and intelligent soul of twenty nine. We took to each other immediately. She told me later she looked on me as a sister, which both delighted and flattered me, for I was extremely fond of her.

Our rented bungalow was right in the middle of a wood with not another building in sight, and part of a large woodland estate called "Inwood" belonging to some rich Americans. At one end stood a huge, lovely house they owned but only used for their summer vacations, standing empty nearly all year. Jean Cookson looked after it as well as our bungalow which was its guest bungalow. The grounds were heavily wooded throughout with cedar trees, smelling delicious — and even better when we put logs on the fire. Jean Cookson was virtually our nearest neighbour living at the other end of the estate, but quite out of sight of our bungalow. As you can imagine we were pretty isolated with only a footpath down to the lane. No cars were allowed in Bermuda with everyone using bicycles, so no garages were necessary and there was no dangerous traffic on the lovely narrow flower-decked lanes. Truly a paradise, the colour and beauty was much too wonderful to try and describe.

Being so near, Jean would walk over to me through the woods with Nicky, her black spaniel, to sit with me whilst we gossiped and discussed any little problems I had. One thing that had puzzled me were some big black elongated "seeds" as I imagined them to be, all along the edges of each room, so I asked her to tell me what sort of trees these had come from. She had one look and let out a loud laugh replying, "Good heavens girl, that's rat dirt!" I said, "Well, they won't be welcome, but I expect it's because the place has been left empty for so long." I wasn't frightfully concerned until that night when the racket started, after we'd gone to bed. The most unbelievable commotion started up inside the wall behind my bed — I declare there must have been a rat fight there. Above our heads in the roof they thundered about, scrabbling, scratching and racing back and forth. Sleep was absolutely impossible.

Early next day I was on the phone to Jean asking for some advice, "Ring up the pest control officer and get him to come round", she told me. Arriving with two huge traps which he put down on the table, this worthy proceeded to tell me how and where to use them, what bait to use etc. I asked him, "But aren't you going to set them for me?" "Oh no", he said, "we leave them for you to do that". Hoping the rats might just go away now they found occupants in the house, I didn't do anything with the traps, but no luck, they just continued their cavorting as usual. I knew I'd have to screw up my courage and tackle the problem sooner or later.

About 7 o'clock the next night Jill and Jocelyn, out playing in the woods called out to me, "Mummy, come and look at this." Going out to see what they wanted to show me, I was aghast. One cedar tree close to the bungalow had telephone wires attached which led on to our roof. I couldn't believe my eyes! A procession of huge rats were high wire balancing their way across the wires onto my roof. Now I knew how they got in. We all picked up stones and bricks, and shied them at these brutes as they tottered along but we didn't manage to knock any of them off. What was worse was they seemed totally unafraid of us. I didn't like that all. Some I could see were decidely pregnant too. Visions of nests of young high above my head didn't improve my frame of mind, and I determined I'd have to get rid of them somehow. Ismay offered to help but I said I wouldn't be beaten and I'd tackle it myself if she'd just come and hold the trap door in the ceiling open for me. The rat officer told me to be sure to attach a strong piece of string to each trap and let it hang down from the trap door. Otherwise, he said, a rat not immediately killed in its efforts to get free would drag the trap into the roof where I wouldn't be able to reach it. Raw bacon made the best bait in his opinion.

Very gingerly I managed to bait the traps and by standing on a chair put them into position leaving the string hanging down as directed. My heart in my mouth as I went to bed, and sleep was impossible as I was waiting for any results from up above. I didn't have long to wait for soon there was a "thump" followed by complete silence! I waited for about quarter of an hour just in case, then got out of bed, removed the trap door and pulled the string. Crashing down came the trap with a huge pregnant rat in it! I felt deeply gratified and not a little proud of myself. Taking the lot into the kitchen I heaved it out of the window deciding to deal with it next day. Ismay's room was right at the end of the L-shaped bungalow, as servants quarters were always built on the end of building, almost like a separate block. Ismay helped me move the rat out of the trap next morning. The following night and on many more I followed the same procedure telling the children not to get up if they heard any thumps and bumps as I would be dealing with it all. They'd often call out to me, "Mummy, the rats must be playing hide and seek behind our dressing table tonight". This nightly pandemonium went on for weeks until one night when the trap went off followed by a succession of heavy bangs accompanied by the most blood curdling screams you've ever heard rent the air. I was petrified! Those screams went right through me and I knew what had happened. With so much use the trap had slackened and hadn't killed the wretched creature but had just caught it. Its struggles and shrieks were utterly appalling. Horrified and wondering what to do, I saw the trap door was vibrating madly with all the thrashing about. Suddenly everything came tumbling down and there hung the trap with a huge, very alive rat struggling, screaming and gazing at me with terrified eyes. I daren't go near it, yet I had to pass it to get to Ismay. Too far away to hear anything, I desperately needed her help and this revolting assemblage was hanging and swinging in the opening that divided my bedroom from the sitting room. I had to get past it somehow.

Eventually with my heart in my mouth I edged sideways past and ran to fetch Ismay. Returning we both stood in our nightgowns viewing this distressing sight. She said, "Don't touch it Madam, it'll bite you for certain." I told her I'd no intention of touching it but it couldn't just be left hanging there. The pathetic creatures staring eyes made me feel quite like a criminal. Finally Ismay suggested we cut the string and she would then take it outside and kill it. "Right", I said, "I'll get the scissors". I cut the string and Ismay took it outside with a suitable log she found in the firegrate. Indoors, I heard her banging and thumping away at it. Coming back indoors looking very concerned Ismay told me "It won't die, what am I to do?" "I know", I replied, "Get a bucket of water and drown the poor thing". Hastily this is what we did. After the deed was finally accomplished we sank into chairs, sighing with relief, deciding a cup of tea was very necessary. I vowed there and then that whatever happened from then on I was setting no more traps. By this time Grandpa had gone back to England of course, so he never really knew anything about this nasty experience.

Our lease on the bungalow was almost up and I knew we had to find another abode. This didn't bother me much except that when I left I knew I'd have to part company with Ismay too. Ismay was such an attractive girl. When she dressed up to go out she was quite stunning in a white sharkskin suit, two tone court shoes and matching accessories. Admirers she had by the dozen, judging by the number of phone calls in seductive, velvet tongued voices asking to speak with her. She usually told me of her admirers and who she was going out with at the time. One she fancied very much, used to bring us vegetables in a horse and cart, and I had quite a few pleasant surprises from time to time, like new potatoes, fresh peaches, etc. This affair came to nothing though. For once I think she was more smitten than he was. However, another I came to meet in very different circumstances.

One night at about two in the morning, I heard loud angry voices — a most frightful row was going on somewhere. Knowing Ismay had been out with a date, I wondered if she was in yet and it was anything involving her. Checking up I saw the light was on in her room and that was where the row was coming from. As she was obviously in some sort of trouble I charged in, dressed in my nightie and pink kimono. The sight that met my eyes proved I was more than right. There was Ismay, her face bruised and swollen with all her clothes torn off and scattered all over the room. Nearby, there was a fellow, head in hands, slumped in a chair. When I could get any sense out of either of them, bit by bit I got the story. It seems that Ismay had been his steady girl friend for some time, even though he was married with six children. The affair had cooled, but on Ismay's side only as she had found herself another fellow. She'd been out with fellow number two but fellow number one had seen this. He followed them home and declared the other man had been invited into her room. Going in himself he claimed he's caught them in very compromising circumstances indeed, and had gone berserk, had a punch up with his rival and then pitched into

Ismay herself in no ordinary way. I pitched into him verbally without pausing for breath, pointing out that Ismay was an unattached girl and could choose who she wished to go out with, whilst he was married with a large family and so on and so on.

Weeping, clasping my hands, almost on his knees, he begged me, "Oh, please don't report me, or I shall lose my job as the lift man at the Bank of Bermuda and my life will be ruined." "On one condition only", I said, "I will promise to say nothing, but you must never never lay a hand on Ismay or annoy her in any way ever again". (I felt like a judge!) "And now you'd better clear off as fast as you can for I don't want to hear of you again, ever."

He certainly cleared off quickly. Ismay jumped up, threw her arms around my neck, sobbing into my shoulder that she would always feel I was a real sister to her. Later I saw the man in town one day. Dashing across the road to me, he shook my hand so vigorously I thought I'd never get free. He just couldn't be grateful enough for my keeping quiet about that most awful night, as he'd been living in dread that I might not. Dear Ismay, when I left the "Inwood" bungalow she went off to America with some Americans who paid her a fabulous wage. She kept in touch for a while, writing to me from time to time.

While looking for another house, a dear old lady who lived next door to Jean Cookson called Miss Alexander, persuaded me to go and live with her in her bungalow. With lots of room she said she'd welcome the children, declaring they would be like grandchildren to her. I confess she seemed a rather old and forbidding looking spinster to us, and though only fifty nine, looked and acted more. The children were horrified. Not wanting to go they put up all manner of excuses. I think her very formal, abrupt manner placed them in some awe. However, she was really very well meaning and liked us, so I was very grateful for her suggestion. She told me I could have the kitchen to myself and tried to put everything at our convenience. But still the children complained. They didn't want to live there even though I assured them it was only until we had found a house of our own, for I'd no idea how long we'd be staying in Bermuda. So we went there and I continued my hunt for a house. When the children complained that Miss Alexander had ticked them off just for leaning their bicyles against her cherished stephanotis, knocking some of its buds off, I knew we couldn't stay for long. But I must say she was very kind to me, and we remained good friends for years and years afterwards, corresponding quite frequently. When at long last I found Ivy cottage she was really upset and begged us not to leave. I explained the children wanted more room, to have all their friends in to meals, etc., and it would be best if I took the house that I had been so very lucky to find advertised in the local paper.

Although dozens of people were after Ivy Cottage Mrs. Alan Smith, the perfectly sweet old lady of seventy who owned it, said she would rather we had it than anyone else for she was determined to let it to English people. English herself, but born in Bermuda, her large family was scattered all over the island. She let me have it very cheaply (at the only price I could afford) although she could have got far more from Americans. Of course this wasn't entirely altruistic of her as she knew very well that they would demand far more for their money than we would.

Ivy Cottage did have a few drawbacks, but we were young and carefree and could accept them fairly easily. The cooking arrangements were far from ideal, and the water catchment a disgrace. The cooker was an oil burning affair, just a paraffin cooker with a small oven. I got used to it in time and even made good pastry on it. All the water in Bermuda is rain water, the white painted roof tops collecting the rain which flows down into catchment tanks alongside or beneath the houses. New homes, I believe, have tanks built under the foundations.

Ivy Cottage. Of many memories, this bungalow was our second home on Bermuda. Not everything about it was pleasant, such as the heavy infestation of fleas and dead animals in the water tank. See text, page 113, for more details.

Despite the problems Ivy cottage was a most delightful and historic old cottage. I heard a man had taken his bride there in 1780, or thereabouts. It had many old and "interesting" features. The water tank for example. A trap door in its side enabled one to peep in to see the water level. One had to be very careful and sparing indeed in using water during the summer months, with articles in the newspaper asking people to be careful. Often there were good rows over some tenants (always Americans) who showered twice a day, running their tanks dry and have to wait for rain to get them refilled. Sometimes water had to be imported but was very expensive indeed.

Jocelyn had a look through the trap one day and came running in saying, "Mummy, there's a perfect white mouse in the water tank!" Looking in myself, to my horror I saw it was indeed a very white mouse. A very dead and badly decomposed, bloated, white mouse floating on top of the water in the half-empty tank! Then I panicked, for looking around some more I saw two dead frogs! This was our drinking water! We boiled it of course, but even so I was appalled. My landlady didn't seem to be alarmed when I told her though, begging her to do something, which she said she would. A week passed and nothing had happened, so I went to see if she had told the tank cleaners to come. As she hadn't, on the advice of my many friends I ordered them to come myself, sending her their bill. The men who came were horrified, emptying the tank bucket by bucket. With water being so precious, the first lot out was eagerly seized by a family of Portuguese for washing clothes, as they took in bits of laundry including some of ours. The last two feet was solid sludge, smelling so foul the men told me they had to smoke pipes while they were shovelling it all out.

I wondered if all this would sever my friendship with my sweet landlady but it didn't and we remained firm friends and wrote to each other until she died in her nineties. Another drawback vied with the tank in its horror. Opening one of the bedroom doors for the first time, a cloud, and I mean a cloud, of fleas pounced upon our legs covering them until they were literally black. I just couldn't believe my eyes and, oh dear me, how they bit us! There were so many of them we had to brush them off our legs, not pick them off one at a time! These fleas infested the whole house.

Once again I got on the phone to the pest officer. "Oh, yes," he said very casually, "Fleas in the onion season aren't at all unusual, some houses have them, some don't." It was a situation I couldn't ignore and, as usual, it was left to me to try and deal with it somehow. I'd heard benzine was a very good deterrent, so I got a huge bottle from the chemist, and scrubbed the floor with it. Suddenly I collapsed, becoming very dizzy, falling about, sick and nauseated, in such a state of collapse I thought I'd die. Luckily the district nurse called to attend to Jill's finger which had gone septic after she'd almost cut the top off whilst opening a can of dog food. She saw me swooning about and said, "Whatever's the matter?" I said I'd no idea, which I hadn't. She questioned me and discovered my efforts with the Benzine and exploded, amazed that I wasn't in hospital, telling me that I had thoroughly poisoned myself. Benzine was a most dangerous substance it seemed. I hadn't known this of course, but I just had to find something to deal with those fleas.

When I felt better I decided kerosene might do it. Half filling a bucket, I got a mop and sloshed it all over the bedroom floor, in between the floorboards, on the skirting boards, just about everywhere. It was a crazy thing to do, and I shudder to think of the fire risk which must have been awful. Luckily no one came in with a cigarette, or struck a match, so I got away with it. It didn't entirely destroy the fleas, but it discouraged them quite a lot. I had to wait until the onion season was over when they gradually faded away as I had been told they would. But it was hell while it lasted.

Bermuda in those days was a most glorious, peaceful place having no cars, just bicycles, carriages and horses. A unique feature was the little train which ran from one end of the island to the other and, to our amused joy, straight through the main street of Hamilton. It really was a godsend as one could cycle as far as one wished then wait at a halt to catch the train. One's cycle would be put in a specially designed van on the end of the train ready for when you wanted to get off again. Jill and Jocelyn went to school in Hamilton on this little train each day. We usually cycled everywhere, with the two dogs we'd acquired seated in the bicycle baskets. One was a Peke someone had asked us to look after while she was in Canada for three months, which we were glade to do. How we came to have the black spaniel puppy I just forget as I had said, "No dogs" as we were only there on a temporary basis, so it wasn't fair on either us or the dogs. But somehow this spaniel had been foisted on us though and I knew when the time came to leave I'd have to find a home for him.

Next to join the household were two white mice the children produced. The first thing I wanted to be sure of was, were they both of the same sex? Oh, yes, emphatically they were, they'd been assured of that, so into a nice strong cage installed in the verandah they went. One morning going into feed them we found over a dozen white mice, not just two. Just as I'd feared, of course. After a week I couldn't bear the smell any longer and another place had to be found to keep them. The previous tenants must have kept hens for there was a disused hen pen and shed in the grounds some distance from the house. With much protest cage and contents were removed to this shed, a dry and safe place with a door that could be closed at night. This scheme seemed very satisfactory till one morning the children came running in, in great distress. I had to go and look at once. A pitiful sight greeted me for some creature had chewed a round hole through the wood, got in and slaughtered the lot except two poor shivering and trembling little mites clinging to the roof of the cage. Naturally, these poor things were carefully cosseted in a shoe box in the children's bedroom after that, I just couldn't refuse, could I! Finally, one day Jill took them for a walk. I'd warned her they'd lose them and they did, for the mice leapt into the hedge and were never seen again.

Of our large circle of friends my closest was Mary Haggerston. She had come out from England with a nanny and three small children for the duration of the war, as most of my friends had done. An American, married to an English baronet, she told me she had lost her first child, a boy, in Egypt, and there was no one to inherit the title for she only produced girls after that. We became very close friends, her oldest daughter Belinda being the same age as Jocelyn, so they got very friendly. Belinda would spend a few nights with us and Jocelyn would be asked back in return, but always refused, although she was persuaded to go on one occasion. At ten thirty that night the phone went and Mary told me, "I've got a little girl on my knee who is crying and wants to go home." "I'm very sorry", I told her, "but she will have to stay where she is as I'm not going to walk through the woodland in the dark to fetch her".

We were deeply shocked when our peaceful paradise was shattered by two tragic events which seemed out of character in Bermuda. We were regularly visited by a friend of mine, a Naval officer's wife called Kathy, together with her small son. They lived in a bungalow on the other side of Hamilton regularly coming over to spend a day with me. Expecting one of her weekly visits, instead of arriving, she rang me in great distress. I begged her to tell me what was the matter. Incoherently, all she could gasp out was, "I can't I can't, something terrible happened in the night". And rang off. Later, I discovered that during the night a coloured man had crept into her bungalow, raped her, and stayed all night, threatening he would strangle her if she called

Bermuda, 1941. A wonderful island where we had many friends, one of whom was Mary Haggerston, an American and the wife of Sir Carnaby Haggerston. Tall and elegant she's wearing slacks which at that time had already been fashionable for quite a while.

out or made any effort to escape. His hands around her throat convinced her that he meant what he said. Even though her next door neighbour was a mere few yards away — she could even see light in their kitchen — she daren't make a sound. Her child slept through the whole affair in the next bedroom. Eventually he left issuing threats about what he would do if he found out she had phoned the police. Of course, as soon as she could she fled to her neighbours, who phoned the police and the doctor.

The poor girl had to go to the police station many times being subjected to the most horrible examinations and interrogations. She had to listen to voices hidden behind blankets to see if she could recognise or identify them. The most terrible aspect of it all was that she had to write and tell her husband of her ordeal, as he was at sea in the Far East. She knew if she didn't tell him he would find out from somebody else, as by now it was plastered all over the pages of the Bermuda papers. While considering how best to do this, her husband's ship was torpedoed and he went down with the vessel, without even knowing of this appalling event. So the poor girl had this grievous loss on top of her own ordeal to bear. For certain, when she left on a ship to England, she carried with her no happy memories of Bermuda.

Not long after this episode, something else even more horrific happened, although not to any friend of mine. A mature lady had cycled back home from dinner at a friend's house one night, along a dark and lonely path beside the railway. She failed to phone her host, as she had arranged to do when she arrived home, to assure him she was alright. As no message arrived a search was mounted soon finding both her cycle, slippery with blood and then her horribly mutilated body, obviously the work of a real beast of a man. Naturally, the newspapers carried all the awful details. The really tragic part of it was that her parents only found out what had happened by reading about her fate in the English papers. After this incident we didn't feel so secure as we had, for the man responsible wasn't caught for long after we had left Bermuda. After his trial he paid the ultimate penalty for his crime, being hanged by the neck until dead.

Jocelyn spent her ninth birthday in Bermuda and I gave a big beach party to mark the occasion. Often, when the moon was rising at a convenient time, we would get together with friends and take a picnic supper to the beach and bathe by moonlight. One night the moon didn't oblige and dusk fell rather quickly. Quickly we gathered up all the gear, Sybil Goldsmith, a friend and nearest neighbour, hastily putting swimming trunks and things into a bag. Picking up what she thought was a sandal she let out a fearful scream for it was a huge crab and had seized her hand with it's claw and wouldn't let go. Rushing to help her, try as I might I couldn't shift it, the brute just hung on. Sybil cried out with the pain as I tried to prise its claw apart but it was absolutely locked on solid, besides making grabs at me with its other claw the while. It was a full five minutes before we managed to get it off. Poor Sybil had a very nasty swollen hand for days.

During the school holidays the house was always full of children. One girl, Sarah Gregg, was particularly popular with Jill as she shared her love of animals. This girl had a horse but, unlike us just there for the war years, the family were permanent residents and could indulge themselves in a complete menagerie. Asked over to tea one day we were in an elegant drawing room with open french windows. Surprised we saw a couple of hens stroll in followed in quick succession by a duck and then a huge goose! No one seemed to mind. Next, to my utter amazement a goat ambled in and started chewing on a nice embroidered table cloth! Even this only provoked a mild reaction — someone just shooed it out. On the way home, I overheard Jill say to Jocelyn, "Wasn't that simply wonderful? I wish we had a mother like that!" Which immediately drew the comment from

me that I thought we had enough livestock already what with
two dogs, rats, white mice, and fleas.

As I had rented Ivy cottage privately and not through an
agent I missed having Jean Cookson drop in to see how I was
getting on, to give me all the gossip and quite often pass on a
complaint she'd received about Jill climbing over Inwood
House's vegetable garden to raid the strawberry beds. The main
house being empty all the year except during late summer, its
vegetable garden was kept in order by a Portuguese gardener
regularly infuriated by Jill's visitations across the garden wall.
He'd go to Mrs. Cookson and say, "It's the big bugger who does
it!" And Jean used to come to me, laughingly reporting,
"Carlene, your 'big bugger' has been at it again", and I'd reply
that I'd have a few words with the aforementioned. But it made
no difference of course. Jocelyn said she was always made to
stand and keep watch.

I feared the time was coming when I'd have to leave this
lovely island and all the friends I'd made there. A perfect
paradise for children, who thrived there, we all felt the same way
about Bermuda. Mary Haggerston's house was where I had
lunch nearly every day whilst Jill and Jocelyn had theirs at school.
I just loved sitting in the sun overlooking the sea and playing
with her gorgeous fourteen month old baby Helias, or "Puss" as
she was always known. Years later it grieved me to read that
"Puss" had died at the age of seventeen. I never discovered why
for by then we were abroad again and had unfortunately lost
touch with the Haggerstons.

But now what I had been dreading actually came to pass. We
were to leave, to go to Jamaica of all places. Grandpa was posted
to the Naval Base at Palisadoes and we got only forty eight hours
in which to pack up and go. We mustn't tell a soul we were
leaving, we were informed, as the movements of ships had to be
kept deadly secret. But this was absurd, for to tell me I mustn't let
it be known I was going had to be utter rubbish. After all, I had to
give notice that I was leaving the house; to ring up the school and
tell them the children would not be coming back; close my bank
account; and to attend to all sorts of sundry odds and ends. In
addition there were three bicycles to sell and a home to be found
for "Sunday", the dog. Besides getting all of this done (without
letting anyone know we were leaving of course!), I also had to
arrange transport for our luggage to be taken aboard ship. And
all in forty eight hours! It took some doing, I can tell you. Mary
Haggerston saw us off, and with many tearful farewells we left
Bermuda for Jamaica.

CHAPTER 13

Jamaica

*Blistering heat and my efforts to keep
cool. A mule train to Cinchona. Tram
rides. Blair's "Ghost"*

The journey down in the troopship Medura was rather dreary
although the children seemed to enjoy it for the ship was
crowded with American personnel who made a big fuss of them,
feeding them with chocolates and cola-colas — entertaining
them generally. Grandpa who had preceded us by air, met us on
arrival. As we stepped into the Naval launch the heat hit me in
suffocating blasts. I thought to myself, "I'm never going to be
able to tolerate this heat". But I had to. For three years. Jill and
Jocelyn seemed to weather it fairly well even though I found it
was too ghastly for words and didn't hesitate to say so.

For the first three weeks we stayed with Mary and Donald
Taylor who became life-long friends. Their bungalow was very
comfortable if such a word could ever apply in that temperature.
They assured me it got a bit cooler after sunset. Well, I suppose
the temperature did drop a degree or two but I must say I hardly
noticed it. As for there being any difference at all between the
summer and winter months was entirely a figment of one's
imagination. Donald and Mary were two of the most delightful

119

people one could ever meet — they making us thoroughly welcome, showing us around, helping us to find a bungalow and get servants etc. I discovered we needed three females and a gardener, despite only having to staff a four-roomed bungalow with verandah. None of the windows had any glass in them, just being fitted with burglar bars. With all my servants I had absolutely nothing to do, not that I felt like doing much as I was so hot all the time. I spent a good deal of time getting out of cold baths to sit soaking wet under an electric fan; when dry, back into the cold bath again to repeat the performance. Why I didn't have more sense goodness knows, but it never occured to me that I could catch cold. I soon found out my mistake for I almost had pneumonia, so I gave that habit up. Instead I took to lying naked on the bathroom's tiled floor, much to cooks' horror as she vowed "I'd catch my death". What demoralised me more was the fact that I got styes on my eyes — as fast as one faded another would appear. Often I had one on each eye at the same time. It got to the point where I felt I didn't want to go out at all to any of the ever-mounting social occasions that came along.

At Christmas time in 1941 we arranged to have a break by going to the Agricultural Station at Cinchona on the top of Blue Mountain in the company of two other families. Quite a large building there were sufficient bedrooms for all of us but we had to take some of our own equipment with us like sheets, towels, and cooking pans etc. The climate there was very different. Breathing was difficult at that height and it took time to get used to the thin air. The journey up was quite unusual. We could go so far by car but the last six miles were by narrow mountain paths. The only way to negotiate these tortuous tracks was on foot or on the back of a mule. Luggage and domestic gear was strapped to pack mules each with a man to urge them on. We all chose docile looking beasts on which to ride and set off. These animals had a nasty habit of seeing something they thought might be food to eat right on the very edge of the path, with a three hundred foot drop below. I was terrified they would lose their footing and go over the edge taking us with them. They were particularly fond of green mangoes, always stopping to munch at them on every available occasion. Invariably, these delights were always resting precariously on the very edge of the precipitous drop.

I was very glad and relieved when we finally arrived safely. There wasn't much to do once having got there except to walk, sit around, talk and drink (which I didn't). I was dreading the prospect of having to go back down to the heat again, without realising what a nightmare the journey back was going to be. A journey I've never forgotten. When all was loaded up the procession of mules began, with the pack animals at the rear with their attendants and our own in front. Grandpa and a couple of other men decided they would walk but I felt rather weary and decided to have a mule like the children. The path was so narrow that there wasn't even room for a human being to pass one by. Slowly one behind the other we trundled along.

The mule I'd been allotted was a very poor specimen that kept stumbling almost throwing me off over it's head and neck. I suspect it was very tired having been used too much for carrying heavy coffee sacks the day before. I complained about this to the black fellow who was leading the mules just behind me. His reply was, "Oh no Missy, it's a very fine animal", and gave the poor thing a whack with his stick. The poor animal lurched forward very nearly having me off! Turning I said, "Don't ever do that again", for directly in front of me were Jill and Jocelyn on their mules. I was terrified that if my mule took off suddenly, it would force them over the cliff edge, there being no room whatsoever to get past them.

After stumbling along uncertainly for a while my mule fell a long way behind. The idiot behind me decided to do something about this and gave my mule a mighty whack across it's rump. It gave one tremendous lurch, shot under me throwing me off to land on my back on top of a huge lump of rock. Luckily I fell on the inner side or I'd have gone tumbling down three hundred feet or more! I thought I'd had it and lay there vaguely wondering if I was going to spend my life in a wheel chair, or worse, for I was in agony and couldn't move at all. Grandpa and the menfolk rushed back and tried unsuccessfully to get me to move. Grandpa decided my back didn't seem to be broken, even though it felt like it, they discussed how they could get me down, resolving to make a makeshift stretcher as I obviously couldn't even sit up.

Somebody had an idea that a collapsed deck chair, strapped to two poles would suffice. Poles were obtained by the muleteers, who went up the mountainside and cut down two trees of suitable thickness with their machetes. These poles were then strapped to the sides of the deck chair, and I was gradually eased on to the contraption. To my distress we hadn't been going long before I most desperately wanted to spend a penny. How this was going to be managed put me in a real panic. I halted the procession and explained the problem to Grandpa, who was far from pleased. He tried to insist that I must wait, but I said I couldn't. My four black stretcher bearers were told to make themselves scarce, and then, as I was wearing trousers not a skirt, I began a series of gymnastics and tactics which I'll leave to your imagination. I have some rather poor photographs of me on the stretcher in one of my albums.

Half way down we transferred to motor transport, but with no ambulance available I was lifted and somehow fitted into the back of a car. Arriving back home I was put to bed, where I stayed for three weeks, just black and blue all over. Ten years or so later when I'd had an X-ray for something or other the doctor asked me, "Do you know you've got a lump of bone out of your spine. Have you had an accident you can remember?" Did I remember? I'll say I did. And I remember lying in bed wondering if I'd ever be free from pain passing the time watching a huge "John Crow" as it was called in Jamaica. A horrible great vulture with its skinny neck would sit on the roof of the bungalow next door gazing down at me day after day. I suppose it hoped that I was going to die! They were the most offensive creatures, forever raiding dustbins and eating anything that had died or looked like dying. Seeing one consume a whole chicken in my garden one day, I dashed at it with a stick, only to have it turn round and hiss at me most evilly.

Delicious fruit was something of a consolation for the unbearable climate, particularly mangoes and avocado pears. Enormous grapefruit growing in one's own garden was a novelty not to mention the bananas and all kinds of other fruits I had never seen before. Still fantastically hot the temperature fell one night to a mere 74 degrees Fahrenheit, and I felt cold! It must have been highly unusual for it only ever happened the once. We had acquired some extremely good friends on the other side of the island who were most hospitable occasionally asking us to spend a few days or even a whole week with them now and then. They had a most lovely house and estate reaching down to the beach at Runaway Bay. Peter and Alice Blagrove were a bit older than we were and had no children. My two were given a most wonderful welcome and loved going there. The Blagroves owned an estate with a great house called Cardiff Hall which they had let to two war widows. We all went there to lunch when we stayed with the Blagroves. Cardiff Hall, had its own chapel and burial ground and I found it most interesting to wander round reading the Blagroves' ancestors names on the burial stones. Peter pointed out one tomb to me which contained his namesake with the legend, "Peter Blagrove, aged 19, poisoned by one of his slaves", dated seventeen hundred and something. The Blagroves owned some fascinating ledgers containing all the names, ages and particulars of their ancestors' slaves, dating back hundreds of years. It was sad to read of the prices they were bought and sold for, their ages, who they married, what children they produced and lastly, when and what age they died. The cause of death always seemed to be "Belly Ache" with this notation appearing in the margin.

The variety of animals the Blagroves kept were a source of joy to Jill in particular. It was here for the first time that I saw black crabs kept in cages and runs like rabbits for the use of the table. Very delicious they were too. One had to be rather careful though as they could easily give one a dose of food poisoning. I unfortunately experienced a dose of this malady, not getting it from the Blagrove's crabs but at another friend's house we called at for lunch on our way home from Runaway Bay. This was the residence of a Major Paton, an old and close friend of the Blagroves, with whom we'd become acquainted whilst visiting them. Although 80, this retired army officer was remarkably fit, healthy and active.

The north side of the island suffered from one great drawback — Malaria. Peter and Jill went out horseriding there, and a week after we got back home Jill went down with a fearful attack. We even doubted that she would survive as she was so ill and delirious, talking nonsense about someone called "George". We never found out who he was. Jill remembered very little about it when she was better. Whilst delirious, almost at death's door it seemed to us, our next door neighbours, Canadians, came over and asked if they could pray for her. Getting our consent they promptly did so there and then on the verandah, which touched me greatly. Peter Blagrove was equally ill with malaria at the same time. Perhaps they'd both been bitten by the same mosquito!

Exquisite green and yellow lizards or gheckos lived in the huge creeper which surrounded our verandah. We used to feed them every day with cake, and pepsi-cola which they simply loved. They got so used to this feast that every day at 4 o'clock they would sit and wait for tea to arrive. Pepsi-cola with the juice of fresh limes was the childrens drink whilst we had tea. Pepsi would be dropped on the floor in spots, the lizards dashing down at once to drink it. This infuriated the stupidly superstitious servants, who vowed these creatures brought them evil. If they got the chance they always killed them. Discovering what they were doing I became very angry threatening that if I saw anyone killing the reptiles they would go at once. That would be evil for them! I expect they kept doing it though when my back was turned. They weren't a bad bunch of rogues really, certainly not as bad as some.

These servants took a bit of getting used to though after having lovely Ismay in Bermuda. But I'd had some introduction to less than perfect servants already, for when Ismay left me to go to America, the replacement I'd had to cope with was her total opposite. A wooden headed dimwit, who, when I told her before a party to wash the lettuce in boiled water, did just that. With water straight out of the hot kettle, reducing it to a steaming pulp.

I taught my old fat black Jamaican cook how to make bread, and she took a great liking to the activity. Afterwards I wished I hadn't shown her, for I saw her one day kneading vigorously with great blobs of perspiration pouring down her chin falling straight into the dough. I never fancied eating it after that.

Why we had wood burning ovens I could never really understand for the kitchen was unbearably hot. We had electricity to run the fridge and so on. All the bungalows had these dreadful wood burning things which the servants seemed to like and get on with.

A form of snobbery prevailed in the kitchen which I found amusing. My housemaid had to be called "Miss Alice" because she was partly white. This was quite usual, I was told, all the servants having to call her "Miss" before her name. There were other examples of a definite "pecking order" amongst the servants. Going out one day I remembered half way down the drive that I hadn't told the cook what I needed from the vegetable woman when she called. Seeing Albert, the gardener, leaning on his fork doing nothing by the gate, I told him, "Albert, go and tell cook I need a water melon and sweet potatoes from the vegetable woman when she calls". Returning I found cook in the kitchen with a face like thunder. I asked her, "Did you get the things from the vegetable woman, Cook?" "No," she said abruptly. So I followed up with, "Didn't Albert tell you then?", to which she replied in a haughty shrug, "I don't take no orders from ze garden boy!"

Thievery of all sorts was rife, many examples of which spring to mind. We'd acquired twenty chickens or so from a friend who was returning to England, and who didn't want to see them killed as they had become almost like pets. They, and their nest boxes were installed in the garden, although two preferred to perch in an avocado pear tree, and we had fresh eggs for several weeks, until one night they all disappeared, except the two in the tree. They went also the following night. Only a trail of feathers leading to a nearby field showed where they'd been carried off by a thief. Other poultry houses in Ardenne Road were raided at the same time, indeed it seemed to be a regular occurrence. Albert claimed he'd heard nothing, which we very much doubted as his bedroom was alongside the hen-house. A very dumb, useless policeman came and spent about two hours taking down all the details at a rate a five year old child could better. We never saw any of the birds again though.

Another theft that vexed me considerably was the loss of a beautiful little crocodile skin travelling clock given me as a wedding present by the Bramelds at Retford. Standing on a small table between our twin beds, it disappeared overnight. I'd say some rogue just put his arm through the burglar bars and hooked it out while we slept. Servants would sometimes claim goods had been stolen, when they'd taken them themselves and sold them to someone.

One instance I thought most amusing. Dennis Hodgson, a bachelor friend living on a big plantation on the other side of the island dropped in on us whenever he came to Kingston, perhaps to have a meal with us. His valet continually told him that his dress shirts, which seemed to be gradually disappearing were at the laundry. Investigating further it transpired the valet had sold them off, and they were now all on waiters backs in the Myrtle Bank Hotel in Kingston!

As Dennis was a magistrate he could tell some hilarious stories. Two men tiptoed into his court behind him one day whilst it was in session, and asked permission to remove the big courtroom clock for repairs. He agreed and it was quitely removed. Neither clock or men were ever seen again. We warned him he'd better watch out or "obeah" (a voodoo curse) would be put on hime. He replied, "Oh, but it has." Riding in through his main gate his horse had nearly fallen over a deep hole, which he found contained a small coffin with an effigy of himself inside all stuck over with pins! He had evidently displeased someone on his staff. But as he remained perfectly hale and hearty, it didn't seem to have worked.

I know of one case where it certainly did though. Dr. and Mrs. Anderson who we knew well had a splendid, smart and athletic black manservant who used to wait at table. Dr. Anderson told us in all seriousness, "Do you know that fellow says he is going to die as someone has put the obeah on him?" We exclaimed in horror at such an idea. "Well, he said, "To try and reassure the fellow I've examined him thoroughly. There's absolutely nothing wrong with him, but he still maintains he's going to die." And dead he was in three months time. A post mortem revealed he was the healthiest specimen one might find with no cause for him to die whatsoever. It's all very puzzling.

After Grandpa left Jamaica I went into a guest house for a time with the children, but eventually I took another bungalow just below our previous residence that had lain empty for a while. Previously the property of a naval officer, Captain Ringrose-Wharton who had an English valet called Blair. One morning there was a great disturbance, servants running about everywhere, all gabbling excitedly. Going out to see what all the fuss was about, I found Blair had hung himself from the branch of a big *lignum vitae* tree in the grounds. No-one had cut him down as this was a job for the police and they didn't arrive for an hour or so! Horrified I ran indoors, only to have my cook come in and try to describe the scene to me in graphic detail with, "Him hung so, Mistress", etc "Be quiet", I said, "I don't want to know how 'he hung' or any more about it". The fact of the suicide didn't bother me though, and it became the second bungalow we occupied in Jamaica. A youth who lived in the next door bungalow and who was rather sweet on Jill used to dress himself up in a sheet at night, creep under her bedroom window to intone in a sonorous voice, "I'm Blair's ghost." Jugs of water were thrown over him if we could catch him. This young man, David Bloomfield, was a keen saxophonist. To our utter amazement when we left he came round very shyly and politely presenting Jill with a small gift. It turned out to be a small brooch in green and gold enamel in the shape of a saxophone. I do hope she's still got it.

A typical feature of the Jamaican scene, was the sight of the overcrowded open sided trams which ran along all the main roads leading to Kingston. I used them quite a lot, partly from necessity, having no car but also for entertainment. The passengers would crowd in and when the seats were full they would hang precariously all along the sides and even lie across what floor space there might be. The loud conversations and back-chat being bandied about between the passengers from one end of the tram to the other were usually most amusing and could be made into a very good book just by themselves! At the various stops, large fat, black women, complete with huge baskets would heave themselves slowly aboard. If the tram should start off before they were completely settled, as often happened, they would at once hurl a furious tirade at the indifferent driver in a broad Jamaican dialect. Following this initial onslaught would come a continuous and lengthy monologue of complaint, until every passenger had joined in, adding bits they thought appropriate. Comments about domestic affairs, their families, the shortcomings of their menfolk, local scandal were alternative subjects of lively exchanges. A woman in the front seat one day shouted to another right at the back, "How is your Mistress today?", the woman in the back answering with just one word, "Dead!", holding up a big wreath she'd had between her knees to illustrate the point!

One had to cling on to the seat in front as the tram's speed increased, rocking from side to side until one feared it would jump the tracks, as sometimes happened. Youths habitually leapt up to cling to the rails on the sides of the moving vehicle, to decamp before any money was required, thus riding free. No-one seemed to mind. Rattling along at speed one morning a loud shout attracted my attention. Turning to look, I saw that one of the huge fat matrons, who'd been sitting too near the edge, had shot off as we rounded a rather abrupt bend, and was tumbling onto the grass verge. Performing a slow somersault, legs well in the air she revealed all! A voice immediately behind me remarked in laconic tones, "Lard, 'tis a mercy she have on her drawers". It certainly was, for exposed for all to see a great expanse of her very voluminous electric blue bloomers! The tram just proceeded on it's way without stopping as if nothing had happened. Luckily, she didn't seem to be hurt much, well protected by all her natural padding, and doubtless just sat there and waited for the next tram! That was Jamaica for you, alright. A typical attitude, adopted in every situation. I found an enormous amount of unconscious humour everywhere, which I enjoyed just by watching and listening.

I certainly couldn't have sat in any public vehicle that wasn't entirely open, so oppressive was the blistering heat. Even in open conveyances the odour of the many bodies was quite overpowering. Everyone continually used large kerchiefs to mop up the rivulets of perspiration that trickled down between their ample bosoms.

When Grandpa was there we had a car. This was much more perilous than the tram as he was always one of the worst drivers I've ever ridden with in my life. After a cocktail party or wedding he was lethal. How he got through over sixty five years of driving without a major disaster I've no idea, but he managed it somehow! We had a few skirmishes, of course, and some very "near misses".

Driving one day down a very narrow lane in Jamaica, an enormous fat woman was swaying along with a huge basket of fruit on her head. Coming up behind her, Grandpa honked but to no effect. Stupidly trying to edge past her when there was clearly no room, he caught the edge of her basket with the car. Over she went and with a scream fell amongst all her fruit and vegetables, saying all sorts of uncomplimentary things as she lay there in the dust. Grandpa stopped and inspected the situation from the car. From nowhere a fellow appeared, and when Grandpa called out, "Are you alright?" (luckily she was), butted in, "She will be for two pounds, Mister!" Grandpa's reply was very typical! And he drove on.

Grandpa smoked quite heavily then, which, coupled with excessive sunlight, caused him to develop a cancer of the lower lip. I remember shuddering as he removed his cigarette carefully from his mouth as it would stick most painfully to this sinister blister on his lip. He was naturally anxious to get back to England where it could be attended to properly and wasted no time in going into Hasler Hospital as soon as he arrived to have it removed. A nasty operation it was too. In hospital for a week, ever afterwards he said he'd no feeling in his lower lip. Fortunately the blister didn't re-occur but it had to be watched for many years. Even after that he didn't give up smoking straight away. Three years later he had a most fearful heart attack through smoking which frightened the daylights out of him. That did the trick, but that is a later story.

Our time in Jamaica was drawing to a close. Grandpa wrote and told us we either had to seize the next opportunity to catch whatever vessel called in. If we didn't we would have to stay on indefinitely, possibly until the end of the war. That event looked a long way off at that time. So we were warned to stand by and expect to be told to pack up and leave on short notice; if we got three day's notice we would be lucky. Also the same absurd procedure had to be followed as in Bermuda, i.e. tell no one, etc. This was just as silly as before as I had a rented house, Jill and Jocelyn were at school, and lots of other reasons. However, the day duly arrived when Donald Taylor rang me up to inform me, "Carlene, there's a boat calling in three days time and you've got to be on it." Knowing this was how it had to be, we got all packed up and sorted ourselves out somehow, with the help of our service friends, within that timespan.

CHAPTER 14

Back to England, via New York

Through minefields and submarine infested waters, enduring winter gales in primitive, overcrowded conditions

We boarded our ship, the Thermistocles with about forty other people from Jamaica, mostly service wives and children. Although I wasn't expecting any sort of luxury I could scarcely believe my eyes when I saw the appalling accommodation and conditions we would have to endure. The ship had come from Australia and was already crowded before it called at Jamaica. The Australian passengers were extremely hostile to us "Jamaicans", quite rightly saying that the ship was full to capacity before we even got on it. We pointed out we couldn't help it, but they remained very surly and aggressive. After their long trip from Australia who could blame them? Below decks the holds were full of Italian P.o.W.'s being deported to England. We were lucky, I suppose to have a cabin at all, a single one for the three of us, six feet by five feet with one bunk and a space beneath. This we had to make do with. Borrowing a cot mattress from Lavender Harrington travelling in the next cabin with her eighteen month old son, I fixed up a bed for Jocelyn on a cabin trunk. Jocelyn was small, but not that small, and her feet rested up at an angle on the "once upon a time" wash basin.

We had no idea how long our journey would take, and were told nothing, only that we wouldn't be served with any meals unless we had our lifebelts on. The ship sailed all alone, not in convoy, the stories floating around of previous trips turning ones blood cold. Enemy submarines abounded in the Caribbean, many ships having been sunk. Horrific stories could be heard of ships being torpedoed and those on the life rafts machine gunned as the enemy wanted no survivors to give away their location. One story told of an entire family, including a six year old boy, being gunned down in this way. Stories like this did nothing to improve our state of mind, but our physical state had to be our first concern, and that was utterly unbelievable.

Meals, such as they were, had to be queued for and were served in three relays. The food, as was to be expected, was dreadful. Looking back, I'm amazed they managed to feed us at all, for even the Captain hadn't been told to expect forty more people to come on board at Jamaica. I remember eating soup like white wallpaper glue, sitting uncomfortably jammed in beside people who, like us, were almost invisible behind the obligatory but really ridiculous life belts. I say this because it didn't take much brain to work out that if we were torpedoed there were nowhere near enough life boats or rafts to rescue so many passengers. So we would have died anyway just taking a bit longer to do it. However, they were adamant about it, no lifebelts, no food, no exceptions.

Only three wash basins were available for everyone on our side of the deck. It soon became clear it was useless to try to get near these after 6 a.m. as mothers were always using them to wash out nappies. Only three loos, too. Corridors were littered everywhere with old banana skins, orange peel, etc., too awful to describe, especially the smell. Our cabin was so small we'd take turns getting dressed for if one had to bend down the rest had to get on the bunk first. Where to hang our own washing to dry, when and if we caught a rare spell when the basins weren't in use, was another problem. String tied across the cabin from one wall to another had to suffice. So there this wet mess would hang to slap one in the face each time you entered.

Insanitary overcrowded conditions soon produced an epidemic of illnesses — flu, pneumonia, bronchitis and tummy upsets. The only doctor aboard was inundated, couldn't cope and said so. Those who kept well went around trying to help those who weren't. No antibiotics in those days remember, so anyone with pneumonia either just died or didn't. Quite simple really. I visited one British family of four travelling from Jamaica all with pneumonia, to try and do something to help. I found it quite pathetic to see the poor mother and three children lying there so ill with lines of wet washing just dangling above their faces.

We struck up a friendship with a most kind, brown skinned, not very dark little Jamaican man. Travelling alone, he came from a well-known, respected and very rich coloured family. To his credit he was going to England to do his bit for the war effort, having volunteered to work in the ammunition factories in Coventry. I thought him extremely valiant to expose himself voluntarily to what was going on in England, when he could have stayed in Jamaica living in the lap of luxury as he was accustomed. He sort of attached himself to us and couldn't do enough to help us. The girls used to call him my boyfriend as he could be regularly seen coming down to our cabin every morning. I had some difficulty living this down. Considering the conditions we were living under this was really hilarious. He'd queue up for cups of tea for us at teatime. Being distressed to see our washing hanging round our faces he offered to fix up something of a line on the open deck above. The weather was foul and all the bits and pieces around our cabin were flying about, as we rolled, pitched and tossed about having to hang on to anything stable. So I let him take my washing to see if he could fix up a line on the open deck. Returning later with a long face and full of apologies, he had to confess that the washing, line and all, had been whipped out to sea never to be seen again. Ironing was an impossibility. Indeed, I never even saw an iron, but this didn't stop some women asking me to referee over a squabble about who had first right to use the one and only iron that was reputed to exist. Anyway, ironing in those conditions? I wonder anyone bothered.

One morning a commotion on deck caught my attention whilst I was getting some air. We'd acquired an escort of three Canadian corvettes. These tough little crafts patrolled the waters to help any passing ship. Seemingly we were heading in the wrong direction for an officer in charge of one corvette bellowed to our Captain through a megaphone, "What the hell d'you think you're doing? Change course at once, you're heading into a minefield!" This gave us a great feeling of confidence, I do assure you! After that it's not surprising that we didn't have much confidence in our Captain. Though I never saw him, he had the reputation of being a very surly and unapproachabe man. One can't blame him I suppose, as he'd already lost two sons in the war and was now in charge of this floating pack of trouble.

Monica, a friend who'd been a sort of Secretary ADC to the Governor in Jamaica, was sharing a cabin with four others, one of whom started having hysterical fits. Shouting and ranting in the night, she'd get up and shriek out, "The boat's sinking, the boat's sinking". It got so bad that Monica told the Captain they couldn't stand it any longer, could he please have her removed as she was definitely going mad. His completely unhelpful, if possibly accurate response was, "Everybody on this bloody boat is going mad, so one more won't make much difference".

One day, to our amazement, a cabin steward actually appeared poking his nose round the curtain (we weren't allowed doors). In a broad Yorkshire accent he said, "How are you girls getting on?", staying to talk for a bit, retailing some hair raising if amusing stores of events that had happened on previous trips. After that call he made quite regular trips to our cabin to see us, not to do anything for us but just to chat. All the cabins were wide open, just like ours. There was no privacy whatsoever, but morale was so low no one cared. I used to tell people, "Do be careful when you come in for you might step on my face", for usually I used to sleep on the floor. Quite often we took it in turns for the bunk, whoever was feeling most ill at the time normally getting preference.

Inevitably we all went down with flu. Jill also developed a most alarming pain in her side which I immediately thought was appendicitis. Desperate, for she really seemed very ill, I went to the overworked doctor and begged him to come. At his wits end he said he couldn't possibly come but perhaps I wouldn't mind if he got an Italian doctor, a prisoner of war, from below decks to have a look at her. Anyone was all right by me so long as they saw to her for she was in awful pain. Presently up came this Italian doctor, with an armed guard and an interpreter. Examing her, he asked me, "Has she ever had malaria". "Yes," I told him, "Very badly about three years ago." "I thought so," he replied, "Its a very enlarged spleen caused through malaria." It seemed nothing could be done but at least it didn't need an operation, for which I felt very thankful.

Due in New York in a few days time the steward told us, "God knows where we've been, at sea for three weeks now, we must have been up to Iceland!" He asked us, "Anything you girls want?" We were always "you three girls". Without hesitation I said, "Yes, there's no loo paper in the lavatory, could you get a roll please?" He hooted with coarse laughter, saying, "Good gracious no, you'll just have to use a bit of stick". Jill's expression when it dawned on her what these three words meant just had to be seen to be believed. She turned her back on him, and I don't think ever spoke to him again.

As we got in sight of New York I relucantly emerged from my hibernation going on deck to look at the harbour and skyline, standing beside a very sweet elderly gentleman who had come all the way from Australia. Chatting, he asked me if I had been to New York before and I told him we hadn't. He pointed out all the buildings for us explaining what they were. "What a charming man", I thought. What happened to him I'll say later.

We went ashore escorted by our Jamaican friend who was most attentive and kind. Knowing New York well, he took us around the places he thought we'd be interested in. Taxis everywhere, which he paid for, super meals at hotels and a shopping spree! At Macy's he couldn't be restrained from buying me five umbrellas just because I admired one of them.

Eventually we were all taken to a big hall where some hospitable Americans had laid on doughnuts and coffee, making a fuss of us generally. At night our lovely Jamaican protector booked seats at Radio City for us all, buying me a lovely orchid on the way there. He even tried to hold my hand during the performance which I thought was going a bit too far. Whilst leaving, Jocelyn was entranced by the fantastic surroundings and engrossed in examining herself in one of the enormous mirrors at the head of some stairs. Missing her footing she tumbled head over heels right down to the very bottom with me frantically trying to catch up with her. Fortunately she was wearing what we all wore in those days, a zoot suit, a sort of skiing suit made of heavy material, which softened her fall, as did the thick red carpets. So, apart from having a very surprised look on her face she completely escaped hurting herself.

We stayed in New York harbour for three days in all, each day going on one jaunt or another, always with our attentive escort of course. One night, walking down brightly-lit Broadway at 2.30 a.m., I remember wondering what Grandpa would have said if he could have seen us. Luckily he never found out about the episode, as I'd never have heard the end of it.

Our New York break over off we went on the most dangerous part of our trip to England, this time in a very long convoy. The January weather did it's worst, with snow storms, gales and waves that threatened to tear the ship apart. Everything that wasn't tied down in the cabin just flew around and hit us. Struggling to the dining room was really dangerous with one being thrown from side to side of the corridor. Everything on the dining tables had to be clamped down. The charming gentleman from Australia whose acquaintance I'd made in New York harbour where he'd pointed out the skyline to me, was going to lunch one day when the ship gave a particularly violent roll. Thrown against the door frame he struck his head so heavily he was knocked unconscious. For three days he lingered on, whilst volunteers sat with him. Then he died. I didn't care for the experience of a funeral at sea, so didn't attend, but Jocelyn and Jill insisted on going. Being in convoy it had to be done pretty swiftly for we couldn't stop or slow down but had to keep pace with the other ships in the column.

I flatly refused to leave my cabin much to the concern of my little Jamaican friend who pleaded with me to go up on deck to get some air. Every day the anti-aircraft guns on deck above us would start firing, and that was enough for me. I didn't want to see it as well as hear it. The weather didn't abate at all, the visibility at times being almost nil it was snowing so hard. Five days out from England we were told never to take our clothes off, and to sleep fully dressed including our shoes. This didn't concern us much since we'd not washed even our faces for days on end, as the water had run out. Literally nothing mattered, least of all what we looked like. On the day before we were due to dock I tried to locate three crates of grapefruit that had been put in my care for someone in England. They'd completely vanished like mostly everything on board. Even the purser had his watch pinched during the trip from under his pillow as he slept. Tablets of soap and tubes of toothpaste had to be hidden carefully, and even then would disappear. Everything like this was severely rationed in England, so I suppose the idea was to grab all one could while it was available.

All of this happened over forty five years ago, and I sometimes think about what might have happened to the people who shared our plight. I did hear that the little Jamaican eventually went back to his homeland to marry an English woman. Monica, the friend who shared a cabin with the demented female, must have died by now, as she was something like fifty then. Whatever happened to the little steward, or to any of them I wonder?

CHAPTER 15

Back Home at Last

Northwood, air-raids, "Doodle bugs"
and rationing. "Silverdale" Privett Road.
Grandpa collapses, and stops smoking

Barry Docks on a wild mid-winters day isn't a very cheerful looking place. Grandpa herded us into a car which must have been laid on by the Navy to take us to the station to begin the long dreary journey to Northwood, Middlesex, arriving when it was pitch black. And pitch was the right word for it. We'd never seen a total blackout before and found it really frightening. On getting out of the train we held on to each other tightly for if we let go for an instant we'd never have found each other again. Cheerful voices told us through the inky blackness that there hadn't been an air-raid for three weeks. Somehow we got to "home", which turned out to be a nice, modern, furnished house Grandpa had rented. It was a joy and comfort to find Mother waiting there for us as we'd been away from England for seven years. I felt a pang when I saw that she looked considerably older than when we left, natural enough as she was now seventy. Her first words to me were, "Good gracious child, you look yellow!" "That's not very surprising Mother after our last five weeks", I replied. Jocelyn took one look round and burst into tears. I felt very like it myself and could sympathise. That very night the sirens went off and we were treated to a first-class air raid. For three weeks every night it was the same. We had no air raid shelter, so either got up and went downstairs or watched it from our bedroom windows. What a most frightening sight it was, with parachute flares floating down, and searchlights making everything as light as day. Shaking with fright I tried to assure the girls that the planes were miles away by now. This was not very convincing when we could actually see the "dog fights" going on directly above us and hear the anti-aircraft guns banging away at them. Remembering that these guns were being operated by girls as well as men makes me proud to have been of a generation in which the women's war efforts were almost beyond belief.

I had to laugh one day when Jocelyn remarked, "You know Mummy, if it wasn't for me you'd be working in a factory." She was right, too, as anyone with children over fifteen, or without a family, had to work just wherever the Government thought fit. One friend, a commander's wife, was told to paint white lines down the middle of roads! I forget if she managed to get out of that one, as one usually put up a protest of some sort if the job was too awful. I must say the thought of factory work frightened me!

Most houses had an air raid shelter built in the garden, sometimes below ground level although they were by no means totally safe, as a direct hit would certainly kill everyone inside. Indeed one of my own old South African friends and her young son were killed in a shelter. People took to almost camping out in their shelters, making them into a sort of underground second home. When all the sirens went they'd all troop down there and brew some tea, staying there until the "all clear", which often meant for a whole day. Personally I thought I'd rather be killed on top of the ground than trapped beneath it.

St. Helen's, Northwood, an excellent, well known and respected girl's school was close by and we got the girls enrolled with no difficulty. I still have a note from the Headmistress saying that as the girls had to spend so much time in the air raid shelters she'd decided to close the school three weeks earlier than usual.

Life was extremely difficult to get used to as I had to face the fact that I now had to cope with everything by myself. An amusing thought in 1988 I dare say, but I'd always been used to life which took it for granted that we didn't do our own cooking, washing up, making fires etc. I was doing something at the sink one day with Jocelyn helping, when she made me laugh by

St.Helen's, Northwood.

A.R.P.   June 19th.1944

During the present emergency we propose to pursue the
following policy:
          As the trenches are across the grounds and Alerts are
likely to be frequent we shall not take the children there
for the present but will continue as far as possible with
normal school.   Those forms which are at the top of the
house, or whose rooms have a great deal of glass, have been
brought to the ground-floor.
          The children will have games and swimming as usual as
long as all is quiet, but will be brought indoors at the
first sign of gunfire.
          Break and midday dinner are served in the dining room
which is reinforced and shuttered.
          This policy of observing gunfire rather than Alerts
will be pursued also when it is time for the children to go
home unless parents notify us that they would prefer the
children to stay here until the "All Clear" is sounded.

G. A. Mackenzie.

Headmistress.

saying, "Now I don't really mind doing this once in a while
Mummy, but surely we shan't have to do it forever, will we?" "I
hope not", I replied. But we've both done quite a lot of it since!
Then it was inevitable, there wasn't any alternative. Somehow in
those hard days I managed to find a woman willing to do the
housework three times a week, bringing her three children with
her. Better than nothing, I thought, and was glad of her help. One
of her children was only a tot of eighteen months.

By the time we'd given them cocoa, and mopped up the
baby's puddles, the sirens would go warning us of a raid. The
poor mite would then cling to her mother's skirt wailing, "No,
Mummy, no", and we'd have to try and comfort it. I felt sorry for
them but not all that much work was done. She was a nice
woman though, and needed the money, always turning up
regularly on time despite all she must have had to do. When the
flying bombs started, "doodle bugs" as they were known, this
little family had a terribly near miss. These fearful missiles began
to appear in June 1944, in fact I think I saw the very first one come
over London, whilst hanging out clothes in the garden. I heard
the drone of an engine and looked up to see what looked like a
plane with fire coming out of its tail. Almost at once the
anti-aircraft guns began firing at it. I thought the pilot must be a
very cool customer, for the plane just kept straight on, not
attempting to dodge at all. Shrapnell from the flak was falling all

around so I ran indoors. A terrific explosion happened only a few seconds later — which didn't amaze me at all, just thinking he'd dropped a bomb. Later I went shopping and overheard a woman in a long fish queue saying, "Did you see that Hitler pilotless plane come over?" I thought, "Pilotless planes? What nonsense these people hatch up." But she was right, of course, and it was the first of many. We got used to the dreadful sound of their engines and would hold our breath while counting the seconds from the time the engine cut out, covering our ears for the explosion which followed, thankful it hadn't fallen on us. We were horrified by the knowledge that these awful bangs always meant the end of many lives, not to mention the injuries. Eventually, they stopped firing at them at all, unless they were over the Channel, where they would fall safely into the water, for firing at them over built-up areas often caused more damage than ever.

One of these horrors came over about four thirty one afternoon, sounding perilously near, so near in fact, that we thought it was probably a fleet of American bombers, so Jill and I rushed to have a look. I'd been getting Jill ready for her confirmation arranged for about half an hour later. Suddenly the noise stopped. We knew what that meant. Then, almost immediately, a deafening explosion. We grabbed each other, shut our eyes and I felt my hair fly up and saw Jill's do the same as the terrific blast hit us. Jocelyn shouted down from upstairs, "Mummy, the loo seat has just lifted me clean off it!" Jill's confirmation frock had been blown to the floor from the chair it had been hanging on, together with other things. Grandpa came in minutes later saying, "That was a near miss, I thought I'd had it and flung myself on the ground along with everyone near me."

Collecting ourselves together off we went to the church for the confirmation service. The blast had hit this building shattering the windows and with rubble about everywhere. I was worried about the roof being safe, and even more by the great slices of glass dangling and wafting in the breeze just held up by torn blackout paper. I was horrified that at any moment this lethal glass would crash down on the children's heads, as they stood lined up in the aisle. The Bishop began his address with, "I feel sure that at this moment no one's mind is on what's about to take place." How right he was. I remember nothing at all of that service, except a lot of helpers sweeping up the glass and rubble, constantly watching those great slices of glass swining perilously from the church roof on ragged bits of black paper. That particular doodle bug caused many deaths as it fell on densely built-up estate of tightly packed houses. Next morning my domestic help told me all the awful details. Her baby had a big plaster across its nose and she had several plasters on various parts of her. The blast had blown their back door clean through the house and knocked the front door out with its impact. They escaped with their lives but many didn't.

We were only in London for a few months more as Grandpa was appointed to the Lee-on-Solent Fleet Air Arm establishment. Once more we began house hunting, but easier this time for we were in the familiar surroundings of Alverstoke. Friends there helped, including putting us all up until we found a furnished house of our own. Our hosts, the doctor who'd brought Jill into the world, and his wife had a huge house so accommodation was no problem. Catering must have been more difficult, of course, and they had to take charge of our ration books. We knew we had to keep ridigly to our "ration" of everything. That's not easy with a large family for one is always conscious that to take too much of anything would be more than uncivil. Children in particular can easily overstep the mark quite unwittingly. However, it worked out all right. I was very grateful for their help and kindness, despite one or two "ups and downs" we had whilst in residence.

Gladly we seized a furnished house which came available in the Bury Road. Only being able to rent it for a few months we had to keep an eye open for something to follow. Grandpa heard of a house for sale, but the owner didn't want to rent it — only sell, and he was adamant on the point. Prices then were fantastically low. In places as vulnerable to bombing as Gosport prices were even lower, houses being almost given away — no one wanted to own a house that might be flattened any minute. So this splendid house, in Privett Road was purchased for only 2,500 pounds. A lot of money in those days, but this house had six bedrooms, all with washbasins, and a lovely parquet floored drawing room. The walled garden had a huge, glorious copper beech tree, which Jill was always climbing to the top, giving me a fit.

A convenient school for the girls was only a mere few hundred yards away. They hated this school, run by a man (unheard of then) for both boys and girls, which my two viewed with great distaste. Although the best we could do it wasn't long before complaints came from the headmaster that Jill wasn't working at all. It didn't help much to find her at the top of the beech tree when he called to discuss matters, especially as she was supposed to be in the middle of exams and working hard.

During our time in Silverdale rationing got worse and even bread was put on ration. Fruit was a rarity, the mere mention of

bananas causing a queue to form up outside of the shop. A ration
book was required for these, one banana allowed per book. I
hatched a scheme by which I sent Jill down for her ration,
followed by me for another and then Jocelyn, to collect three
times over. This didn't work though as the chap in the shop
looked at Jocelyn and said loudly, "Oh, no, you don't your two
sisters (??) have just been in and collected your lot. Beat it!"

Our arrival at Silverdale House was unforgettable, as we had
no furniture at all. Sale rooms we scoured for anything usable.
Never having had a home before, we found we were entitled to
buy "Utility" furniture on a "points" system. Although new this
was of the shoddiest kind. No one would give it house room
today but we were delighted to be able to buy beds, blankets,
chairs and so on of any sort. I bought a most beautiful
secondhand dining table at a sale. That table, and all the rest was
left behind when we sold the house.

Sitting on the bottom of the stairs waiting for the man to
unload the rest of the downstairs furniture, Grandpa suddenly
gave a shout, a gasp and then collapsed. Jill and I with the
furniture mens assistance got him upstairs and on to a bed. One

look at his blue face was enough, and I flew to the phone (mercifully left installed in the house) and got hold of Doctor Berry. Coming right away, I ran upstairs with him, frankly not knowing if we'd find Grandpa alive or dead. Doctor Berry gave him something to breathe which he took in dreadful gasps and which restored him somewhat, easing the pains in his chest. From being blue he turned a deathly white. "This is it", I thought, "he's going to die", and I was paralysed with horror. Bill Berry waited until the dreadful spasm has cleared. Then he read the riot act in no uncertain terms, beginning with "Now, you listen to me. You're a doctor and you know these things. If you ever smoke one more cigarette I'll wash my hands of you. And I mean it". Grandpa smoked quite a lot and had done so since he was seventeen. After about two weeks in bed he sat up and said, "I want a cigarette." "You're not having one", I told him, "You know what Bill Berry told you." His reply, "I don't care a damn what Bill said, I want a cigarette. If you don't bring me one, I'll get up and get one myself. And I might well drop down dead if I do that." Jill and I conferred behind the door. "What are we going to do?" I hit on an idea I thought a reasonable compromise. "Let's give him one but cut a piece off the end first. He won't notice and it'll at least shorten his smoke." We were right, he didn't notice. So we kept this up until one day I was busy. He was calling out for a cigarette so I told Jill, "Take him one but don't forget to cut it first." She did, but cut off too much and he noticed, bellowing out, "What the hell are you playing at." etc. etc. What a row there was! "Right", I said, "I'll go and tell Bill Berry you're trying to kill yourself." This did it. With great reluctance he cut down to about three cigarettes a day. Later, very gradually and painfully, he cut out all smoking altogether and wasn't fit to live with for six months or so. But from the day he decided to stop he kept to it somehow. After the withdrawal symptoms had ceased, he got to such a stage that he couldn't bear to be in the same room as someone who was smoking. This detestation of smoking stayed with him for the rest of his life.

After he recovered, his next job was in Singapore. As soon as he arrived he was put straight into hospital. His coronary had left him in no shape for tackling a new job in that climate and back home he came, naturally very depressed. After a few weeks rest he was re-appointed to the RN Hospital at Simonstown, South Africa, as Senior Medical Officer. As this was a three year posting, we decided to sell Silverdale complete with all its contents. After all, we had no reason to believe that we would be coming back to the area, and didn't want the responsibility of letting it. Many tried to persuade us to rent it to them furnished. We nearly did so as someone offered us such a good rent. Then we discovered by chance they planned to share it with about three other families which made up our minds for us very quickly. All our possessions would have been useless by the time we saw them again. Selling up was the only practical solution.

Grandpa went off to South Africa, leaving us behind to find a buyer for the house. Our sailing date was fixed so I was in a panic to get a buyer and get all the legal matters cleared up before we sailed. Packing was complicated by Jocelyn getting a most awful dose of chicken pox a couple of weeks before we were due to sail. She was really ill and distressed and I hated leaving her in bed on her own while I flew around making all the arrangements. Just for variety I also had to take Jill to the Portsmouth Royal Hospital for treatment of a painful verucca on the sole of her foot. Things are never simple are they?

It saddened me to leave the house and the area for many reasons. Margot, my sister, was not long back from Mombasa where she'd been an acting matron, loving it there until struck down with a severe attack of amoebic dysentry. Invalided home, after sick leave she was posted to a light job as Superintending Sister at the nearby RN Base, Tichfield. We spent many happy days together, but I could see she was far from well. We'd seen a lot of her, and this would now come to an end. Jocelyn recovered and our departure grew nearer. Mother and Margot came to stay as well as Schoie, my dear old friend, a principal of the Gilmer School of Dancing where I'd trained. I well remember her wonderful energy. At sixty six she could still outskip Jill aged only seventeen!

CHAPTER 16

Simonstown —The Second Time Around

Baboons, snakes and haunted houses.
Jill and Jocelyn become very popular
with many admirers

Margot and Mother saw us off from Southampton on the Carnarvon Castle. Converted to a troop ship during the war the ship was still in its wartime condition when we travelled on her again in 1946. Waving goodbye I never dreamt I'd never see Margot again, and when I saw Mother she would be unable to speak, paralysed by a stroke.

We shared our cabin on the packed vessel with two of the many brides on the ship on their honeymoons and an old lady of eighty-six. Naturally enough the honeymoon brides were very disgruntled because they, like everyone on board, had been separated from their menfolk. There were dozens and dozens of children aboard of all ages, mostly young. Mealtimes were a nightmare of squeals, shrieks and howls. I heard one poor mite screaming she wanted to go home and I could well understand the poor child's feelings. Most of the brides had only been married a week, their husbands going out to jobs in the copper mines. Their thought was to start a new life in a new country. I often wonder how they got on and felt sad for them having to leave their parents and families behind in England.

The old lady in our cabin was a sweet, aristocratic old dear. Certainly, it wasn't a good idea to put her with young people, but accommodation was so limited so I suppose there wasn't much option. A good sailor having done the trip before, we tried not to look at her when she got ready for bed for fear of making her embarrassed. She wore a wig and, from the awful smell, was a bit incontinent. A "bit of cloth", produced each morning to be hung on the bottom of the bunk, was definitely very suspect. Tactfully, I asked our steward if he could do anything about it. Taking one sniff he gasped, then picked it up most delicately and threw it overboard. That night the poor old dear began looking for it, asking us, "Have you seen my bit of cloth?" Feeling very guilty we disclaimed all knowledge of the disgusting object, pretending to help her look for it everywhere. Mostly the passengers were very friendly. We usually sat chatting on deck with a man who was returning to South Africa. Enquiring if we had been there before at all recently I told him, "Well, yes, we have been there before, in fact, my youngest daughter (pointing to Jocelyn) was born there." "Oh, really, so you've been there in the last seven or eight years then?", he said. Jocelyn's face was a study, for at nearly fourteen she took a very dim view of being mistaken for a seven or eight year old!

Grandpa's greeting on our arrival wasn't the sort one would expect after three or four months absence. In loud and expressive tones he launched into a tirade over not having heard from the solicitors about the sale of the house — why hadn't I done more about it — I'd had enough time, etc. etc. It rather dampened the joy of arrival.

South Africa the second time round was far from the happy experience I remembered when Jocelyn was born and those years before and after. Our house was now the one the Twiggs had occupied during our first visit. Somehow I always felt her presence to such a degree that it never felt like my house at all. Continually, I half expected to find her two objectionable yapping dogs called Roughy and Coolie to come dashing out snapping at my ankles. Even though the house was half way up the mountainside with lovely views I can't say I ever liked it much. The garden, if such it could be called, was carved out of the hillside in terraces in an attempt to keep the dusty soil from sliding down. Nothing much would grow except the things that were already there and could tolerate the shallow impoverished soil, constantly blown away by the south easterly winds. James, our pleasant but very dim gardener was useful at catching snakes but not much else, knowing absolutely nothing about gardens.

On the second posting, 1946-48 we used the
Senior Medical Officer's house, which had
been occupied by the Twiggs on the first
occasion we were at the Cape. A much less
pleasant house, where we experienced some
disturbing events.

Very proudly he told me one day that he'd pulled all the grass out
of a big flower bed. When I went to look I nearly passed out. The
"grass" was a bed of freesias just coming through!

Within a week Grandpa had fixed up a school for Jocelyn. In
fact, if I remember correctly, he'd arranged it in advance so
perfectly that she was due to attend the very day after we arrived.
She was much aggrieved by this and protested, especially as for
the first time Jill wasn't going with her. Now seventeen, Jill saw
no reason why she should go to yet another school, so, after
arguments with Grandpa, he agreed to let her go to Capetown for
a secretarial course. She did extremely well, getting herself
qualified and a job in one of the Government Offices. Jocelyn
found that being taught by nuns in her convent school, attended
by most of the Naval officers' daughters a bit alarming at first.
Soon, though, she became very attached to them finding out how
very human they are and fun too, having a very happy time,
keeping in touch with them for years afterwards.

Soon it became obvious that Jocelyn had throat trouble,
having recurrent tonsilitis. A Capetowns ear, nose and throat
specialist was consulted and on his advice we arranged for him
to remove her tonsils and adenoids at the Simonstown RN
Hospital. As a treat and to give her a boost after hearing this

nasty news I bought her a lovely little suede jacket she greatly fancied. I wonder if she remembers? I was much relieved we lived so near the hospital for there were so many nurses and VAD's eager to look after her. The operation drained her dreadfully though, and after a few days she was carried on a stretcher down the steps to our house and put to bed, looking absolutely dreadful. It took all of three weeks to get her on her feet again. Her convalescence over, the result was truly marvellous; no more awful colds, glands gone and now able to enjoy life fully.

The Pomfret girls were extremely popular, so popular that midshipmen and young lieutenants would have to make arrangements much in advance if they wanted to escort them to any of the dances or do's! Wails of, "So and so has asked me to go to such and such a dance and I've already promised so and so and can't get out of it", became very familiar. Life was indeed full for them.

I'd suffered from allergic rhinitis for some years but it was made much worse by the South African dusty conditions and high winds in South Africa. Often, hardly able to breathe I'd get up at night and walk on the stoep outside the bedroom gasping for air, at four or five in the morning trying to get breath into my lungs. No inhaler could find a passage through my solid nose; it was almost unbearable. On one such occasion I suddenly noticed that the garden was absolutely full of baboons. They hadn't seen me and so I could watch the amazing sight of about thirty animals of all sizes and ages ravaging the garden. A big wire fence easily six feet high round the garden hadn't deterred them. A huge male sat on the highest terrace obviously acting as lookout, while the rest were busy plundering my garden. Three apricot bushes had half ripe fruit on them which these brutes were stripping off, eating the ripe side of the fruit and tossing the rest over their shoulders. Tomato vines were pulled up by the roots, bulbs being unearthed and chewed. Furious I let out an angry yell and they all dashed off over the fence, climbing it with ease. The mothers grabbed their young ones who seemed reluctant to go and weren't unduly alarmed by me. It amused me to see how they grabbed their young and with a swift smack, just like a human mother, toss them onto their backs to leap off over the fence. Two adolescents on a lower terrace were engrossed in turning up my rockery stones and hadn't heard the commotion. Coming up, they were puzzled to find all the rest had disappeared, till I clapped my hands and shouted as loud as I could when they too made a wild dash for the fence. Troops of baboons would come down most nights to the waterfall by our house to drink and play — we often heard them barking.

Baboons have always been a pest in this part of the Cape. My cook told me that as a tiny baby she was grabbed from her crib outside the house by a baboon down from the mountain who then leapt up onto the corrugated roof with her tucked under her arm. Her mother's cries brought help but no-one dared chase it for fear it would just throw the child down. Eventually the beast was coaxed down and one of the men made a grab and got the baby back. I fully believe this story to be true as baboons have been known to grab babies, especially a female that's lost its own baby.

One of the few houses beside the winding road up the mountain to our house belonged to friends of ours, a sweet old couple, a parson called Martin and his wife. He was close to eighty but still took services in the church. One time, Mrs. Martin rang me, gasping, to tell me of a frightful experience she'd had. Calling from the foot of her stairs to her brother in a bedroom that breakfast was ready, to her utter amazement a big baboon appeared. She screamed, her brother immediately appearing behind the baboon. Feeling trapped the creature leapt past her into the dining room and kitchen where it dashed around and around in circles, upon the table and shelves scattering pots, pans and breakfast things. In its panic it left a trail of poo over absolutely everything. Fried eggs, bacon and marmalade were spread across the walls. Her brother managed to shut it in the pantry until they could open some doors to let it out. Hearing of the damage it had done and utter chaos it had caused, I was realy sorry for her, but secretly I confess I was rather amused, but managed to say, "At least it won't come back in a hurry." How wrong I was — the same baboon was up in her fig tree the very next morning eating the figs.

Baboons often raided the VAD quarters about thirty yards from our house, stealing fruit from the sideboards. One of the girls told us she came home late one night to find a big baboon sitting at her dressing table eating grapes and spitting the pips out at his reflection in the mirror! She shouted at him and threw the nearest thing to hand at him. This happened to be a box of matches which he promptly threw straight back!

My pet aversion was snakes, the most prevalent there being extremely dangerous cobras and puff adders. Lifting up stones or slabs in the garden to root out slugs and observe all other weird creatures has always been a favourite pastime of mine. I soon learned not to do it in South Africa though, for one day I found a neatly coiled cobra under a stone not at all pleased at being disturbed. Another cobra was discovered under a back door mat. Much worse, a Naval officer's wife was taking a bath when a huge cobra, presumbly sleeping on a beam in the ceiling and disturbed by the steam, fell down with a plop right into the water beside her. Screaming she leapt from the bath and ran straight into the road stark naked. An incident that was talked about for quite a time afterwards, as you can well imagine.

Cook was a dear old soul with a large grown up family, one of whom was in her twenties and dying of TB. I was happy for her to sleep at home, fearing the infection would be brought to our house. Eventually she left us altogether. That left us with Yon, a sort of half Indian, half native from one of the islands in some way attached to the Navy. He did a bit of everything, cooking, housework and any chores necessary. When cook left he developed into being a full time cook. If that's what one could call it. He wasn't very pleased at having to cope on his own but not having long to go at the Cape, (the RN Hospital was closing down) Grandpa said he wasn't going to bother getting another cook. Yon must do the lot! Sometimes he got very drunk on Saturdays, so I'm told, but I never saw him really drunk. But to this day, the smell of milk burning reminds me of him. His efforts at cooking were truly atrocious. A young doctor taking Christmas lunch with us opined that the pudding sauce was more like shoe polish. I had to agree! Whatever went into it I'll never know. Poor old Yon (only thirty or so really) took a very dim view of life when Grandpa went away for a few days, asking me if he could have the week off. "Why?", I asked. He said, "Well, when Captain's away Miss Jill and Miss Jocelyn give too many parties". He didn't like to say I gave too many parties for them, which is probably what he really meant. True, our parties were a bit limited when Grandpa was there, so we made hay while the sun shone.

All told I don't look back on my time out there, the second time round with any nostalgia. In June 1947 my sister Margot died. For many months I had been getting distressing and dreadful accounts of her illness from the Sister who was looking after her in St. Bartholomew's Hospital where she was being nursed, and where she herself had indeed trained years before. It shattered me to read in a copy of the overseas Times that she had died on June 1st and was to be cremated on the 7th. I hadn't been told, and to read it in print came as a terrible shock. I was very conscious and worried that my mother was all alone in this grief. I couldn't do anything though, as we were due to return to

England in only a few months time. It was all deeply harrowing. Dying at 44, Margot had perished from a rare and complicated form of cancer developing from amoebic dysentry contracted whilst she was in Mombasa. It grieved me that I couldn't have been with her, but when her release came at least it ended most terrible suffering. At least she died in the hospital she loved.

Margot had become a Superintending Sister equivalent in the Navy, I believe, to the rank of Lt. Commander. A more efficient, capable and respected member of her profession would be hard to find. Never married, hospitals were her life and total interest, she loved her job. All her adult life was spent in hospitals a consequence of which I'll mention more later.

However, life had to go on. Jill and Jocelyn, now at a most fascinating age, were my life. We never, ever had any problems with what in these days is so stupidly called "the generation gap". They never threw adolescent tantrums, had weird hairdo's or dressed like clowns from a circus act as young people do nowadays. Enjoying life to the full, they shared their fun with us, so much so that I look back on their teenage years as being the happiest of my life. Admirers were without number with never a dull moment, the telephone ringing constantly. Their only problem seemed to be how to avoid overlapping their dates. I never worried what they would be doing when they were out with their "dates". All their escorts were delightful youngsters, midshipmen or lieutenants and though the greatest fun to be with, never dreamt of taking the sort of liberties that are so commonplace today. Not that there were no wild parties! I used to love to listen to what went on — but it was always good clean fun. Today's standards don't shock me, I'm merely disappointed to think that so much is missing for youngsters now. So often I find that young people who have been going out together for months seemingly enjoy a sweet, romantic relationship, have actually been living together for months. Then, before long, they separate only to take a similar course with other partners. How can they begin to understand what the word *ROMANCE* means when they get down to a basic urge so soon?

The Neethlings were an extremely nice Africaans family with whom we became very friendly and who lived a short distance away down the hillside, Mr. Neethling being the chief magistrate. Their son Andrew, a very good looking, tall, hefty chap with a wide smile, was very sweet on Jill. Jill couldn't stand him though, and I felt sorry for him watching her expression change to a "po-face" as soon as he appeared. Never able to disguise her feelings, I can always tell at once how she's reacting.

LUNCHEON

Friday, 28th November, 1947.

Flag Lieutenant		Cdr. P. J. Milner-Barry, R.N.
	17	**15**	

Captain (E) A. F. Dobbyn, R.N., (Ret.)	11	21	Mr. E. F. Craggs
Mrs. Westall	18	20	Mrs. Burnett
Major P. G. Burnaby-Atkins, M.C.	19	12	Surg. Captain A. A. Pomfret, O.B.E., R.N.
Mrs. Craggs	16	8	Mrs. Abbott
Commander-in-Chief	7	6	Field Marshall The Rt. Hon., The Viscount Montgomery of Alamein, K.G., G.C.B., D.S.O.
Mrs. Pomfret	1	5	Lady Moody
Lt-Col. G. S. Cole, O.B.E.	24	4	Major-General W. H. E. Poole, C.B., C.B.E., D.S.O
Mrs. Cuthbert	10	3	Mrs. Dobbyn
Captain E. G. Abbott, A.M., R.N.	2	9	Captain W. J. C. Robertson, D.S.C., R.N.
Lt-Col. J. C. Westall, R.M.	13	22	Cdr. (S) A. S. Burnett, R,N.

	23	**14**	
Captain van Wyk			Cdr. S. A. Cuthbert, R.N.

A Luncheon Party. When Field Marshall Viscount Montgomery visited S.A. to inspect the troops in 1947 a luncheon party was given in his honour at Admiralty House. A photograph (above) was taken afterwards in the gardens, in which all the guests were positioned to his requirements.

Whenever Andrew asked her out she was always "very busy". Their large rambling, single storey house was called "The Residency" and had a number of cells beneath it, built long before, but still occasionally in use. The first time we were in the "Cape" living in Sunnyside, the Junior Commander's house, we were very disturbed all one particular night by a commotion coming from the Residency cells. A female caught soliciting at Seaforth and locked away for the night, fought, yelled and screamed all night long. As we heard it so clearly I hate to think how the Neethlings got any sleep at all.

So haunted was the Residency that it was mentioned in the local newspapers a number of times, many very strange things happening there.

Passing the kitchen door one day Mr. Neethling noticed an old woman wearing a black shawl standing there with a big basket on her arm. Once indoors, he told his wife, "Go and see what that old woman wants. I've told the servants they mustn't leave the outside gate unlocked for people to wander in as they please." Investigating, she found no sign of the woman, and the gate locked on the inside, so no one could possibly have left the yard.

On another occasion Mrs. Neethling and her sister, staying with her at the time, were resting after lunch in their respective bedrooms. No one else was in the house and all was quiet. Suddenly they were roused by a woman's voice calling loudly, "Is everybody dead here?" They both jumped up and went out on the stoep or verandah that ran alongside outside the rooms each saying one to the other, "Did you say that?", both replying, "No, wasn't it you?" Both were amazed and mystified that neither of them had said anything, for both had heard it clearly and there wasn't a sign of anyone else about.

All houses in South Africa have these wide stoeps both upstairs and downstairs. It was very lovely in hot weather to sit out for drinks and look at the gorgeous views over the bay. Our house had particularly magnificent views. On arrival there I told the girls to chose which bedrooms they liked, Jocelyn taking one at the front, and Jill one to the back (as it had washbasin which she rather fancied). Grandpa and I had the main bedroom at the far end. No-one else lived in the house, for Yon slept in the Naval quarters and cook slept at home, so I was puzzled when Jill asked me, "Mummy, why do you come and rattle my bedroom door handle in the middle of the night — why don't you come in if you want something?" But I hadn't done anything like this! A few weeks went by and she asked me the same question again, this time saying as well, "Now don't say you didn't come and bang on my door last night, because you did." I vowed I'd done nothing of the sort. Persisting, Jill went on with, "And I keep hearing a very funny noise above my bedroom ceiling some nights." "You dream too much", I told her, "If it's anything at all it must be the water tank or a rat". All there was above her ceiling was a perfectly empty room except for a chest of drawers, one iron bedstead and nothing else. Really, I paid no attention to these odd remarks of hers. Eventually one morning she said, "Now look here, Mummy, you don't believe me I know but next time I hear this noise above me will you come along and listen?" "Yes, all right", I said, "I'll do that." And forgot all about it. Fast asleep one night, in she came, shaking me awake saying, "Come Mummy, come now and listen in my room." I staggered up and went along with her. She got into bed whilst I sat on the edge of it listening. Nothing. I began to get chilly and said, "I can't hear anything and I'm cold. I'm going back to bed." She begged me, "Not yet, Mummy, just wait a little bit longer please." So I waited. Then, suddenly, I heard a most eerie and astonishing sound, one I'll never forget. It was as if a heavy sack or body was being dragged laboriously, bit by bit, across the floor, with brief pauses on account of its bulk. I just stared at Jill, petrified and she gasped, "Now Mummy, now just you tell me that that's the water tank or a rat." Recovering after a few seconds from the initial shock I said, "I'm going up to the attic to look." She said, "Oh, no, don't go up there." "I must, I must", I told her. Though I was terrified I ran up the stairs and flung open the door. There was nothing, not a sign of a thing that could possibly have caused it. The room was untouched, thick with undisturbed dust. Nothing had moved in there for months. I kept quiet about this incident as no one would have believed me anyway, but had to agree with Jill that there was something that defied explanation.

Not long afterwards when we were about to leave the Cape, Yon brought in my breakfast one day with the local paper. On the front page was "Disturbance again at the Residency". Casually I said to Yon, "I see things have been happening again over at the Residency." He replied, "Yes, Madame", but lingered a while, so I added, "Well I'm glad nothing like that happens in this house, it's much too uninteresting and ordinary." He replied, "Do you think so, Madame?" "Why yes", I said, "I do. Don't you?" Looking a bit uncomfortable he answered me with, "Well, this house is supposed to be haunted." "This place haunted, by what and whereabouts?" "Miss Jill's room, Madam, you'd never get any of the maids to sleep in there." My mind flew back to what I'd heard — the door that rattled, the knob that turned in the night, the strange dragging sounds. Not saying any of this I asked him to tell me more. It seemed that a maid had hanged herself in that room and it had been closed off for a long time. He'd been in and seen the print of bare feet in the dust round the bed. He added that the previous Surgeon Captain, a bachelor, used to have his meals in the breakfast room which, if the door was open, looked across the foot of the stairs. One day whilst having his meal he saw a figure hurry past the door and up the stairs. He called to Yon, "Go and see who that is, Yon, one of the sick berth staff might be looking for me." Aghast at all this, I told Yon, "Don't mention a word of this to Miss Jill as she is in that bedroom and we're leaving in only three days time." He promised he wouldn't.

In the car on our way to our ship at Capetown I turned and asked Jill, "You know how you complained about your bedroom one way or another?" "Yes" she said, "What about it". Exploding with laughter I told her it was haunted! I wish you could have seen her face. "There", she said, "I told you about it and you wouldn't believe me, would you?" Then I told her everything Yon had related to me. It's strange but Jill has always been the one to have odd experiences like these from time to time, although Grandpa had one very odd experience I'll relate later.

We sailed for England in the Capetown Castle. The journey was relatively uneventful except that the Pomfret family cleared all the prizes for the table tennis tournaments! Grandpa won the men's competition, I the women's, with Jill coming second, and Jocelyn third. It was, as the presenter said at the time, "A real Pomfret benefit!"

CHAPTER 17

Briefly Back Home Once More

Problems with mother. Jill gets engaged

On arrival home we went to stay with some old friends in Plymouth, Mick Devane, a very Irish Surgeon Commander, and his wife Nell. They treated us most hospitably although I think Jocelyn may have had other ideas.

Quickly, I tried to contact mother. As she wasn't on the phone herself I range her friend at the farm nearby, and was horrified to be told that Mother had had a terrible stroke, was confined to bed, unable to move or speak, and being cared for by this kind neighbour. Of course, I fled to Notthingham, or rather the little village of Lowdham nearby, as fast as I could, taking Jill with me. We installed ourselves in Mother's cottage and went over every day to see her. It was all so harrowing that I don't like to think of it to this day. Her doctor seemed to me to be neither helpful or sympathetic, assuring me that Mother would never be able to live alone again.

I had a real problem here, for as yet we had no idea what Grandpa's next appointment would be. We just didn't know where we were. Jill and I up in Lowdham unable to judge whether Mother would get better or not, and Grandpa with Jocelyn at the Devanes in Plymouth. What to do with mother's cottage was another problem that loomed high on my list of worries.

After some weeks we heard Grandpa was to take charge of the RN Hospital at Portland, a very nice big house going with the appointment. As Mother showed no signs of recovery we decided the only thing to do was to transport her down with us to Portland. Her cottage would have to go, and her favourite bits of furniture be transported to Portland. Afterwards we'd try to work it out from there. Mother was quite furious, in so far as she was able, when she discovered these plans, and it was sometime before she would as much as speak to me, even when she could. I could hardly tell her that the doctor had said she wasn't going to get better and that there was nothing else for it. Grandpa and Jocelyn moved into the house in Portland, whilst I disposed of the cottage and the furniture etc. we weren't taking to Portland. Mother was moved down in an ambulance I'd obtained, Jill and I travelling with her. What a nightmare of a journey that was. Jill refused to ride inside as Mother kept needing a bedpan, sitting up in front with the driver and attendants. I was deeply upset, for poor Mother spent most of the journey crying. Eventually we got to Portland at the end of a long, long journey, never to be forgotten.

Jocelyn's sixteenth birthday, June 9th 1948, wasn't exactly a howling success but the best we could do in the difficult circumstances. Grandpa and Mother had never got on anyway, and now it was very dicey at times. She was very well looked after though, as we had plenty of willing VAD's and nurses at our disposal. Gradually she improved eventually getting back on her feet. Then, not unnaturally, boredom set in for we'd taken her out of her own environment and she was now among strangers. Our extensive social life didn't help matters either. After some discussion Mother relucantly agreed to be looked after as the sole guest in a private home in Portesham that seemed suitable, run by what looked like a very pleasant body. From the start though it didn't look like working out for Mother told us she spent too much time alone. Her host was a keen member of the Woman's Institute, always out or jam making for this or that event. In short, Mother didn't like it there.

Going to see her one day, on ringing the door bell I was aghast to be told, "Your Mother's gone." "Gone?", I said, "Gone where?" "Well she took a taxi back to Nottingham", was the reply. "What address has she gone to?", I asked. "Oh, she didn't leave any address, she just ordered a taxi and went!" I was quite frantic, having no idea where to start looking for her. I didn't want to contact the police but there again I just hadn't any idea where to start. I have nightmares to this very day in which I'm hunting for Mother in Nottingham. Eventually I tracked her down somehow only to find she was in the process of buying a house! I wrote and begged her to abandon the idea, to come back and live with us while we sorted things out. I told her, "Get a taxi and come!" Thank goodness she did as I asked.

By now she had improved greatly; with her hair permed she looked in much better condition. Mentally and physically in much better shape, the three weeks she spent with us were very successful. Mother was now seventy four, and quite agreeable to be moving into a most excellent guest house we located on Weymouth front right in front of the pier. This comfortable establishment was run by an ex-matron purely for elderly but active people. It was stressed though that if a resident became ill no nursing would be available. Mother settled in very well and really liked it making some new friends of her own age including an old clerygman called Pickard Cambridge and an Admiral's widow etc. The food was good and very well served. At last things seemed to settle down and go on pretty smoothly for a while.

Jill became engaged to Charles Hodgson getting married four months later in April 1949. A most lovely wedding in Weymouth with a reception afterwards at the Dorchester Hotel. Mother brought her friend with her and though she looked frail, she enjoyed it all. About now we heard that Grandpa's next appointment would be in charge of the RN Hospital in Bermuda. This was deliciously exciting but slightly marred by the fact that Jill wouldn't be coming with us this time. We'd never been parted before and of course she wasn't even twenty yet.

Grandpa flew off to his new appointment in Bermuda and the Portland house was given up, so Jocelyn and I had nowhere to live. Jocelyn squeezed into Jill and Charles' flat and I was lucky to be offered a home with Jane Twomay, a great and dear friend, in the very top flat of a block right opposite to what was then the Variety Theatre, Alexandra Gardens. Jane was an absolute darling — about three or four years older than me — and we got on wonderfully together. She had a miserable little killjoy of a husband who seemed to hate to see her enjoy anything. Cheerful as a cricket somehow she tolerated his everlasting grumbles and grouses. They had no children and I thought he was thoroughly and completely spoilt. Jane was a heavy smoker and also suffered from asthma with a most appalling cough. Thin as a whippet but with energy galore she insisted on bringing morning tea to me in bed, speechless with coughing. I scolded her saying, "Jane, you shouldn't smoke, you know you'll be ill if you're not careful". She always laughed if off with, "Oh, I'll be fine, it's just when I get up". But she was dead in less than two years all the same, dying suddenly whilst having treatment for asthma in a London hospital. They were about to discharge her next day and found her dead in bed. I was deeply upset, no need to say.

All went well with mother for six months or so until one day I got a phone call from the doctor instructing me to "Come at once." The diagnosis was cancer of a most acute kind, and she had to have an immediate operation. I was quite frantic. The doctor told me she couldn't possibly live the four months to Christmas.

To cope with the situation as best as we could Jocelyn and I took a flat right opposite the hospital gates while Mother was having her operation. Grandpa kept writing to us to ask when we were coming out to join him in Bermuda. We had to wait, of course, to see how Mother got on. After six or seven weeks of very slow recovery she began to talk about being able to live on her own again. This alarmed me, having the doctor's adamant word for it that she'd got three months to live at the most. She insisted though and pressed me to look for a flat. Fortunately I spotted a heaven sent opportunity in the evening paper, in the shape of a flat in St. John's Terrace opposite the church just off the sea front. Going to see it, I found it couldn't have been more suitable and we saw her safely and comfortably installed there with kind people both above and below who promised to keep an eye on her. Jill lived close by in Dorchester Road, and by now was expecting Roger. When we had gone off to Bermuda, Jill made a habit of calling in on Mother, writing to me reporting on how things were going. Mother, to the amazement of the medical profession, lived not only for the three months they'd predicted, but for another three years!

CHAPTER 18

Bermuda Again

But not for long, then back to the UK.
Unexpectedly the family acquires
another member

When I felt it was safe to leave Mother, Jocelyn, Betty and I sailed for Bermuda on the liner SS Bayano. Betty was a cook at the RN Hospital and leapt at the chance of coming out to Bermuda with us. She got on with Grandpa all right, waiting until his back was turned before letting fly with the most colourful language to herself or to anyone who might be within earshot. Some of her varied names for him are quite unrepeatable. Jocelyn and I doubled up with laughing but couldn't deny she usually had good reasons.

I foresaw that a few complications were inevitable as she was a most beautiful and fascinating twenty nine year old divorcee. It wasn't long before the ratings wives got together protesting to us that their husbands were chasing her in every way possible, and she wasn't doing a thing to discourage them. Knowing Betty I could well believe it, but both Jocelyn and I loved her and there seemed little we could do anyway. She was in her element. Beautiful beaches, dances and parties at which she always knew she'd be the belle of the ball, and of course, always surrounded by men who were eager to ply her with gifts and

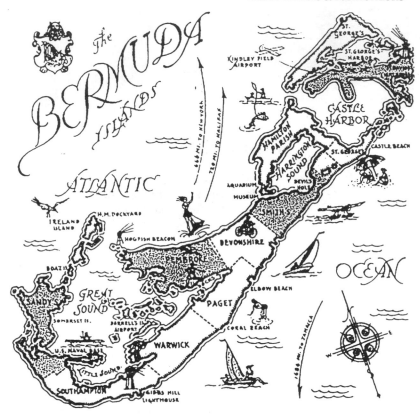

The illustrated map of Bermuda above is a copy taken from a pottery title I was given by Jean Cookson, one of my dearest friends, whilst on the island in the 1940s. During our first visit, we lived in Inwood Bungalow, Paget East, and then moved to Ivy Cottage, Paget West. When we went back in 1949,the posting was to the Naval Hospital on Ireland Island in Somerset Parish. All the places mentioned mean a great deal to me and hole some very special memories.

favours. Where or how it all might have ended I dread to think. All at once we heard the RN Hospital was to be closed though and we were to go home. Then exciting news came that Roger, Jill's first baby, had arrived the day before my forty second birthday. I felt very unwell that very day but at first thought that it was only the excitement of the news that had upset me. In the days that followed I got worse and worse eventually becoming so ill I couldn't leave my bed. As we were due to sail for home in ten

FYFFES LINE

S.S. "BAYANO"

*Sailing from Avonmouth Docks, Bristol
for Bermuda and Jamaica on*

Thursday, 6th October, 1949.

PASSENGER LIST

Commander   .   Captain R. A. Thorburn, R.D., R.N.R.
Chief Engineer   F. Lowry.
Chief Officer .   G. M. Roberts
Chief Steward   W. S. Eggbeer.
Surgeon . . .   J. S. Meighan, M.B., Ch.B.

ELDERS & FYFFES, LIMITED
15, STRATTON STREET,
LONDON, W.1

October, 1949

KELLY

PENISTON

POMFRET

POMFRET

KENNALLS

SPENCER

SWANE

Mrs. E.

Mrs. L. R.

Mrs. D. C.

Miss J. L.

Mr. M. A.

Mrs. M. L.

Mr. D. O.

days time, matters got very complicated. Doctors came and
looked me over and prodded me, Surgeon Commander Flannery
from next door putting it around that I had cancer. Getting on
board the Queen of Bermuda is very hazy. Jean Cookson was
there to see us off and looked at me with a sympathetic eye; what
she heard I don't know. At New York we had to tranship to the
Mauritania. I refused the offer of a stretcher saying I could
manage with help. I saw nothing of that trip, much to Grandpa's
annoyance who reminded me the Queen hadn't paid 40 pounds
a day for me to eat dry water biscuits and milk. Hot milk at that —
something I wouldn't touch normally.

At first we stayed with Jill and Charles in their small rented home in Bedhampton. I didn't want to greet her with my ailments as she didn't look too strong herself and had obviously been working terribly hard to fix up a room for us all. Baby Roger was absolutely lovely. When Jill asked if I'd like to bath him I felt very panicky, for I hadn't bathed a baby for eighteen years. He was only three weeks old, and I was feeling so ill, I'd liked to have died on the spot. Bravely I said, "Of course, I'd love to bath him", and as I gently lowered him into the carefully tested water he let out screams and began to squirm and struggle. Jill watched nervously and I suffered some awful moments thinking I'd done something wrong.

After a couple of weeks we managed to get a flat in Hayling Island. The house belonged to a Surgeon Captain whom we'd known many years before. His widow had now let off most of the large house as a flat which we took over. Grandpa didn't much like her and liked her son even less. A metropolitan policeman, he came most week-ends and I think rather resented the fact his mother had let the best part of the house and they had to live in what was left. For myself I was getting to a stage when I'd have really liked to die as I felt so ill. No one had diagnosed anything yet, so Grandpa got me into the Portsmouth Royal Hospital for observation. To tell the truth I couldn't have cared less where they sent me. I was put in an open ward with all sorts of pathetic sights whenever I opened my eyes. Which wasn't very often. I came to now and again and asked for cocoa without milk. With raised eyebrows the nurse asked me if I usually drank it this way and I said, "No." I remember looking at a sheet of paper at the foot of my bed which read, "a tired looking woman, otherwise healthy!!" Considering how I felt I considered this most unfair. Doctors paraded round me for a week and finally I was inspected by a small, very dour Australian gynaecologist. He didn't waste any time in conversation, swiftly getting on with the job making only one terse utterance, to whit, "Six weeks pregnant, good afternoon." And walked away while the sister and nurse fell about laughing. I can't say that I saw much to laugh about.

We moved from Hayling Island as soon as we could and took a house at Southsea, Nightingale Road, very near to the Queen's Hotel, in a most uninspiring area. Tall boarding houses stood to either side of our small but unique little house, very old and formerly a farm house very many years before. Less than half the height of the lofty houses next to it, it sat huddled in a dark sort of alcove, the sun never touching it. To say it was cold and damp would be a gross understatement. Clothes and shoes grew mouldy in every cupboard and drawer after only a few days. The one and only fireplace blew clouds of smoke back into the room the moment a lump of coal was put on it. This was the depressing set-up I came home to when I left the nursing home with three week old John on Christmas Eve, 1950.

John was born on December 2nd 1950, right on the expected time (the only occasion he has appeared on time ever since). I was, of course, expecting a girl. When I confidently asked the doctor, "It's a girl, isn't it?", I was taken aback by his response. "Well", he said, "It's not you know, it's a very large boy." I was more than amazed as I'd never imagined myself the mother of a boy. He was more than welcome. I did feel rather proud when later on, Matron took him around to all the other mothers to show them what a baby should look like not forgetting to mention he was the largest they'd had and his mother the oldest! I was forty two and three quarters, not exactly very young to produce a baby his size. My first glimpse of him when I came to was to see him lying in his cot with a huge red setter dog with its paws over the side, licking his head! The doctor would have had a fit if he'd seen a dog in the delivery room, never mind half inside the baby's cot. Matron calmly announced this animal always christened babies this way and was very fond of them. This wretched dog, Brandy, was still there six years later when Nicholas, Jill's 4th, was born in the same nursing home. Owing to the stupidity of the staff there I was made to do "exercises" with the result my back suddenly went. By the time I was due to go home I couldn't even lift John from the cot, the agony was so intense. The night before I left, being Christmastime, the Matron had staged a treat for the patients, and a large crowd of carol singers plus harmonium were installed right outside my door on the landing. They started operations about seven o'clock that night and made the most appalling row — howls of Silent Night and Good King Wenceslas reverberated through the building making every baby start to cry. I was very thankful to get away from there. Even Nightingale Road seemed peaceful, pleasant and desirable after that.

So that Grandpa wouldn't be disturbed, I slept in the back bedroom. The view from the window was lovely. It looked directly down into a hotel kitchen and as they started early so did I. I could see the breakfast being prepared and believe me it was lucky the guests couldn't have seen it. Fingers were used to flick bacon from plate to plate plus other unhygenic habits. I found it all quite entertaining.

I managed to find a little fifteen year old girl to help me in the house. She was useful to run errands and take in the washing from the line, peg out nappies etc., so long as someone was there to direct her. While bending down to take something from the trunk one day my right leg seized up. I couldn't straighten my leg and my knee swelled to the size of a football. The doctor took one look and said, "My God, it's a thrombus", and whisked me off to the Naval Hospital at Haslar. The doctor there decided it wasn't though, but that it was rheumatoid arthritis. My main concern was that I'd left my baby in the hands of Grandpa and a fifteen year old girl. The only time they bathed him before I left for the hospital, the poor child let out such a shriek I daren't imagine what they were doing to him. However, for months I was in Haslar, being given every known and unknown drug, until I threw the expected reaction, which I did, and a few more they didn't expect. I reacted as I always do to drugs. Very unfavourably. I was even asked if I'd write an article for the BMJ on my progress and the effects of all this variety of drugs. One in particular called Butozolodin had killed half a dozen people. I've been resistant to penicillin ever since they gave me overdoses of it — to no avail of course. I found it quite humiliating to be lifted in and out of baths and pushed in a wheel chair to physio-therapy.

Back at home Grandpa was coping and advertising for nannies. He got plenty but they never stayed with him for longer than a week. One who came for an interview, was promptly dragooned into holding the baby and coming in the car to Haslar, so that I could interview her! I quickly recognised her type when she said she'd expect to have complete control of the baby etc. Not likely, I thought, I'm not having the same experience I had when Jocelyn was a baby.

Grandpa came to see me daily and did little to relieve my anxiety. Somehow he made me feel the whole situation was my fault, leaving me in tears more than once.

Cortisone was one of the many drugs they used on me. Apart from blowing up my face like a football it created in me a rather "don't care" attitude to life which I badly needed at that time. Months later on when I got back home I had to face yet another imminent move. John had forgotten what I looked like by now and didn't like the look of me at all. He turned to Nanny which pleased her, as it would. When she left, so did his cot eiderdown, his cot pillow and a lot of baby clothes. I was frantic about the eiderdown as it had only been lent to me by a friend whose children were half grown up and was a treasured possession. I explained my awful predicament to her and got another made as exactly as I could in replacement, but of course it could never really replace the original which had such sentimental value.

All this time Jocelyn had been out in Bermuda in what was apparently a very nice job but came back home again in the early spring of 1952. I delayed going into a nursing home in Southsea to have an operation to rectify yet another problem I'd developed until she got back. The internal adjustments needed proved to be quite the most awful thing that ever happened to me. Theoretically it was called a "repair" but, as my dour Australian specialist told the sister, it turned out to be more of a "reconstruction" than a repair. I still had my rheumatoid arthritis of course. In the hope of getting the very best advice Grandpa took me to Harley Street to see a specialist. After giving me a thorough going over he took Grandpa aside and told him I'd get progressively worse to end up in a wheel chair, never to walk again. I didn't know this at the time, so it wasn't my worry. Luckily, as time would show, he couldn't have been more wrong.

Soon we moved to a comfortable modern home in Bedhampton, Jill living only a couple of miles away. She already acquired baby Eve, a little sister for Roger, and was soon expecting Caroline.

Jill contracted German measles soon after her pregnancy with Caroline began, in fact before she even realised she was pregnant again. Roger got the disease at the same time. The potential side effects caused me more worry and sleepless nights than anything I can remember, and I got no comfort from the doctors when I made enquiries to try and reassure myself. That waiting time put years on me. I hoped Jill didn't realise she was pregnant when the measles struck. She told me later she did know but thought I didn't, and so refrained from saying anything. Caroline was born on January 9th 1953 in Chelmondiston, and was a lovely healthy baby until she was three weeks old. Then the problems began, for she couldn't keep any food down. The cause was not entirely unheard of in babies but needed an operation to put it right so she went into hospital in Ipswich. More worries, but she recovered perfectly.

Grandpa was now appointed to a post with the Admiralty in London so we moved yet again. I'd got a Welsh girl, Ethel, as domestic help before we left Bedhampton. Twenty one and though dim, she was willing and pleasant. She couldn't do much for John but I was walking again and didn't need so much help. But it wasn't that easy for once when I took him out in his big pram my knee gave out. I fell flat on my face, the pram up-ended and baby shot forward but was luckily strapped in and came to no harm. I persuaded Ethel to come to London with us, even though she didn't fancy the idea. She ended up hating it as much as I did, and went back to her Aunty in Southsea after only six months. While she was with me in London I swear she saved my life and John's too, quite literally. I had a most horrifying experience in the kitchen one day; I still go icy cold when I think about it even now. Whilst frying sausages for lunch, I went into the pantry for something. John, about two and a half at this time, rushed up and slammed the door behind me. With no latch on the inside I was trapped! Ethel was on her day off, and there was a pan of sausages on the stove in imminent danger of bursting into flame. The kitchen would have been an inferno, and no hope for either John or I. The pantry window was so small I couldn't get my head through it. I yelled, shouted and pounded on the door and on the window. I was frantic for I knew no one was likely to hear me, neighbours being much too far away. Now, I don't believe in chance. Somewhere there is a design, which I don't profess to remotely understand, no one could, but while I was hysterially beating on the door and listening to John excitedly jumping up and down on the other side, obviously thinking it a huge joke, I heard Ethel's voice. She had come back to collect a letter she had intended taking to the post but had forgotten, and she saved the situation. Since then I've made a habit of always looking on the inside of the doors of rooms like pantries or airing cupboards to make sure I could get out should a similar situation arise.

CHAPTER 19

Our Last Posting

Mother dies. We leave the Service

We had only been in London a month or so when it became clear that Mother had not long to go. Going to stay for a week I saw how frail she'd become, even though she battled on, dressing herself each day despite taking half an hour to do so. I hated to leave, but assured her she must send for me if she felt the need. Six weeks later she did so. I went to her staying until she passed away on August 11th 1952. In bed for the last fortnight she remained fully aware mentally to the end, kept free from pain by the doctor's injections. Wonderfully good to her he told me his own mother had died the same way. Mother's lifelong interest in clothes continued until literally her last day when she directed me to find a copy of Vogue in a trunk, so she could show me something she'd ear-marked for me.

I think I've inherited mother's acute memory which stayed with her to the last. She enjoyed recalling events from her early years and I more than enjoyed listening. On her last morning she told me again of a most wonderful experience she'd had as a small child. I never tired of hearing this story which she remembered in vivid unvarying detail.

Six years old, she lived with her very young parents in a remote farmhouse in the depths of the Derbyshire moors, with no other dwelling for three miles, the nearest town being Glossop. Mother loved the wonderful surroundings but naturally found it rather lonely. Her father was away a lot, I believe in the police force in some capacity, and as the eldest child was company for her own mother rather than the two babies that had followed her. I imagine she was a very mature and serious little girl.

They got used to never seeing a soul from one week to another, but didn't get used to the very strange happenings that took place in and around the building.

Mother says she was unconcerned, merely puzzled, when about once a month there would be an urgent knocking on the door, but on opening it there was no one there. Her mother was frightened though, and my own mother was told to answer the door whenever these loud and persistent knocks occurred even though no-one was ever there. She remembers saying, "But Mama it's no use going to the door, there's never anyone there." Mother says she was never alarmed — she had no idea there was anything to be alarmed about, and got quite used to it happening knowing that when she went to the door the knocks would stop.

Every night they would go out to lock up their chickens to keep them safe from the foxes that abounded in the open countryside. On their way through the fruit garden one evening mother suddenly saw a little girl in a white frock with waist length fair hair walking slowly between the blackcurrant bushes, looking down at her feet. Delighted she shouted, "Oh Mama there is a little girl over there," and while her mother said, "Where, where?" she pulled her hand free and ran up to the little girl. Reaching out to touch her the child just vanished, and mother was reduced to tears with disappointment for all her mind was on, was how lovely it would be to have another child to play with. Her own mother, terrified, ran indoors and locked the door. She'd seen nothing but knew my mother had. Her father, who didn't come home often anyway, wasn't very interested in their tales. Once though, feeling unwell, he had decided not to return to Glossop that day and lay on the settee resting. When the urgent banging on the door began, he jumped up whispering, "If it's for me, say I'm in bed ill", and started upstairs, but Mother told him, "It's no-one Daddy, it often does this and there's no one there". "Rubbish", he said, "someone go to the door". There was no-one there of course, and after a while he came down and searched all the outside buildings and grounds, but of course, no-one could be found.

After that he was adamant they must sell up and move. Mother says her poor mother was overjoyed, by now almost a complete nervous wreck. Even mother herself didn't know all that had gone on, but knew her mother had run three miles to the next farm in her nightgown and bare feet one night to collapse on their doorstep. Somehow the farmhouse was sold with never a word mentioned of anything strange happening.

Nowadays if a house is haunted the estate agent has to be told, but then I expect it was sold privately and not through an agent. For a certainty no one would have bought it if they had known of all the strange happenings. A year after they left the new owners wrote asking if there was anything strange about the house, as they had had some disturbing experiences! I don't know how they answered that one. Mother told me that when she was older she realised she had undoubtedly seen the spirit of a child, but didn't find it at all alarming. After my father died in 1921 she always hoped she might see him again. But, much to her disappointment, never again for the rest of her life did she have any other experience of that kind. She was quite unafraid of anything like this, calmly asserting she'd happily stay alone in a haunted house. "It's the living that can harm you", she'd say, "Not those who have gone".

I do wish that when she passed on I'd known all that I do now. My grief would have been so much less. I could have given her so much comfort and assurance. Then I had only orthodox religion to fall back on — and how very inadequate that is! All those trite sayings and quotations, oh dear, how meaningless they are. But then I was still several years away from the spiritual awakening that changed my life for the better.

Grandpa came over to Weymouth for the last week of Mother's life and shocked me greatly by booking seats at the Harbour Pier Theatre for an Arthur English revue on the very day she died. Even though I might not have felt like it, I wouldn't be shocked now. It was his way of getting me back to normality. Mother I know would have understood my love for her was in no way diminished by this unusual gesture. I never think of her laying in an unmarked grave in a cemetery in Weymouth. As my Mother, she will be forever with me forever at all times, most especially when I feel I need her most. The hasty funeral left me feeling numb but back on the train to London we went, for life just had to go on. John was with me, but won't remember anything of the episode for he was only twenty months old then and of course has no memory of her at all.

Our next move was to Plymouth but not before going to Buckingham Palace to see Grandpa get a CBE to add to his OBE!

Our final naval residence — Plymouth. The large house, bottom centre,
with its big garden and curved frontage onto the creek was our last
naval residence. Grandpa was S.R.A. in charge of the Naval Hospital in
the centre of this aerial picture. The creek has long since gone, filled in
now the site of a housing estate! Hospital buildings around the square
included wards for Officers and Other Ranks, specialists working in
the large houses nearby. We did much entertaining, receiving H.R.H.
Princess Alexandra, Lady Mountbatten, Lord Hailsham and many
others.

How exciting it all was! We were overjoyed at his promotion to
Surgeon Rear Admiral and the prospect of him being SRA in
charge at Plymouth.

It was simply wonderful to be back in a system I had always
been used to, lots of entertainment, a staff to look after, meeting
up with old friends from bygone days. And it would be like this
for three whole years! Life was full of interesting incidents and
people, going to parties and dances. Of course it was a bit sad in a
way for we knew this would be the last part of life within the

Service. When we finally left though Grandpa would only be fifty seven and I forty nine. So there would be a lot of life left to be lived and enjoyed, but oh, never in quite the same abundant style.

During this period lots happened to the family. Jocelyn married and we welcomed an army son-in-law into the family. We now have five fine grandsons from that match. Jill who was expecting her fourth child, Nick, spent much of her time struggling from house to house on her own. Jill and Charles had bought a modern house near Havant where Jill was installed to await Nick's arrival whilst Charles was away in South America. I went to be with Jill for the birth having to get a taxi in a great hurry one day to get to the Nursing Home in time.

Roger had been born at the Naval Nursing Home on the front at Southsea, but Jill had used another well-recommended home to have Eve. It was an unfortunate choice for the Matron went off to the races and got very drunk, afterwards throwing a party right above Jill's bedroom. So for Nick's arrival she decided to go to the same place as where I'd had John.

So Jill now had four children all under five years old, and they moved to a big rambling house on the edge of Emsworth in Hampshire. Charles was still in the Navy and had done a spell in Singapore leaving Roger at prep. school and with us during the holidays. That was marvellous for me as I had two boys instead of one and I was young enough to be active and take them on picnics and fishing etc. When they returned from Singapore it became obvious the marriage was crumbling. There's no point in dwelling on whys and wherefores here, suffice it to say that Jill was abandoned to cope with and bring up all four children on her own. From then on she devoted all her energies, time and interest to this rather unruly lot. An excellent job she made of it too, never remarrying or forming any of today's "meaningful relationships" either. A self sufficient stoic then and now, whilst seeming the total opposite — and eye catching to men in every way. I know of quite a few who couldn't understand that they were welcome so long as they kept their distance — and a good distance at that!

On leaving Plymouth when Grandpa retired, we decided to go and live at Exmouth. An old bachelor friend there, Admiral Sir Philip Enright most pleasantly offered to find us a house. This he did, finding one less than three hundred yards from his own where he lived with his unmarried sister. Also we discovered a very good prep. school right next to us for John, not yet seven, who they accepted as a day boy. Grandpa, who had no

intention of retiring for good quickly got himself a nice little job
with the Medical Eye Centre. This not only kept him away all day
but also gave him an interest in life.

I had the garden and John to look after so life didn't seem too
bad. Our lofty, elegant house was the larger part of an old but
attractive early Victorian residence. Inhabited by an eccentric old
lady before us, I was told she'd kept hens in the upstairs rooms.
One day a fire started in an upstairs room and the fire brigade
finished up chasing hens flying in all directions. After she left a
builder turned the derelict building into two nice houses. Ours
faced south enjoying lovely views and having the larger part of
the garden. I had extra windows put in on the south side so we
could see right across to Starcross. The guest room at the back
had the best views but as it was only a single room it was
normally unused.

Grandpa was generally very testy often seeming to pick a
quarrel just for the sake of it. He'd always been inclined to do this
and I usually took little notice, just putting it down to the fact he
found it very hard to adjust to a life outside the Navy. One night,
after getting into bed, an argument began about something
trivial. A bad cold I had made me unwilling to talk on and I said
as much. He flew into such a tizzy, announcing he'd clear out and
sleep in the spare room. "Right," said I, glad to get rid of him. Up
he got and off he went taking his pillow and eiderdown with
him. Gratefully I fell fast asleep. Some time later, I know not how
long, he came thundering back into the bedroom yelling at me,
"What do you mean by coming into my room, pulling my hair
and rocking my head back and forth?" Half asleep I didn't quite
grasp what he was saying, but he repeated, "You've been into
my bedroom, pulled my hair and woken me up. I know you did
it, it's no use denying it for I can still feel where you pulled at my
hair." Awake by now I hotly denied his allegations; but I was
very puzzled. He was so adamant I'd done it, that he fetched his
pillows back and vowed he would never again go into that room
under any circumstances. And he never did. To explain the
incident I tried all the usual theories. He dreamt it perhaps.
Maybe a bird had come into the room. But nothing fitted. His
story stayed the same and he stuck to it. Needless to say he forgot
everything about his argument.

Some time afterwards, I noticed a most fearful smell
apparently coming from under the door of the self same room.
Investigating, I opened the door and the stench that met me was
awful — it seemed to be coming from the door frame and from
underfoot. Ah, I thought, a dead rat or something and arranged

to get it looked into. The odd thing was, the smell would last about ten minutes and then go away completely. This I couldn't understand. However, to be sure we got the floor boards up, but found nothing. I didn't say anything to Grandpa. One day when he was at home and I'd gone up to put some clothes away in the linen cupboard, and this stink was issuing from the spare room, I called to him, "Come upstairs, I want you for a moment." "What for?", he said, grumbling as he came. "Oh, just a moment, come here will you" I said. Crossing the landing he stopped and said, "I'm not going in there, I told you I wouldn't ever again." And so on. "Please", I implored him, "Just come nearer for a second." He came and I flung open the door. Reeling back as the odour really struck him he exploded, "Good God, what on earth have you got in there?" "Nothing", I said and tried to tell him it would be gone in ten minutes. This convinced him more than ever that he'd never set foot in that room again.

It wasn't only Grandpa and I who noticed this smell. A dear good soul who assisted me in the house had come in to help me make up some curtains and a bedspread. We were working with a sewing machine set up in that very room, when I left her briefly to get a tea tray for the two of us. Returning, she said to me, "I hope you won't think it's me, Madam, but there is a most terrible smell in here and I can't understand it." Sure enough the smell was slowly seeping into the room. I then told her about the other events and how this smell came and went for no reason. She was as puzzled as I, for this was a most delightful little room, sunny and with the most enchanting views.

Long after we left that house Grandpa didn't care to discuss the awful experience he'd had. If pressed, he fully admitted to it all and quite seriously too. Whether it was the old lady who used to live there had come back and disapproved of him I don't know. But I smiled to myself and thought of mother! They had never got on very well — she never approved of him and not entirely without reason, I'd say!

CHAPTER 20

We Move to Our Final Home at Chard

Only a year and a half later, to our chagrin, the prep. school next to us closed down departing lock stock and barrel to Kent. No other school nearby had any vacancies, so once again we had to move, this time to Chard, Somerset, where we had found a well-documented prep. school in the private Schools Book, which boasted all the advantages of being a home from home with every known activity and food second to none. It was inspected and a house sought. Unfortunately one house I took a particular fancy to wasn't for sale, although I kept harping on about it to Grandpa's annoyance. He scolded me for not keeping my mind on the number of houses the agent had given us. Despite this, each time we passed it by I'd say, "That's the house I'd like."

House hunting around Chard, I'd picked up a local paper and was studying this and some estate agents leaflets. With sheer disbelief, I saw the house I wanted so much advertised in both the paper as well as in an estate agents particulars. I couldn't get over to Chard fast enough and inside the house, called "Passlands" to look it over. We knew another couple were due at three o'clock to make an offer for it. Whispering to Grandpa, "If you don't buy this house I'll divorce you", we looked it over. I was particularly impressed by the kitchen. The fine view of the open countryside across the fields with cows in them I found quite enchanting. I said to Grandpa, "Tell them you want it!" He felt the same way as me, so immediately reached agreement with the vendors to buy it. The other would-be buyers arrived minutes later, but were too late as we'd already clinched the deal. I always vow I was meant to have that house.

Moved in, we repainted all the brown woodwork white and enthusiastically planned a new garage and greenhouse etc., although Grandpa's enthusiasm for improvements faded drastically over the time we were there. We lived there for twenty five years in all, until he died in 1984 when I moved out and the house was taken over by John and Mary.

I'm happy that Passlands is a family home once more, to hear children's voices and see the old labrador ambling about. I know they all love it. John has his childhood memories there and it touched me deeply to see Mary enthusiastically decorating and renovating much needed areas I always longed to have done, but

"Passlands", Chard. Our home for many years from not long after Grandpa retired from the Navy until he died in 1984, when I moved to Tatworth and Passlands was taken over by John and his wife Mary.

John: John Stephen Pomfret — b. 2nd
December 1950, our only son. In this picture,
taken in Passlands, John is with his wife Mary.

Grandpa steadfastly refused to do anything about. John who
married twice, now lives in Passlands, with his second wife and
two stepchildren, whilst his own daughters live with their
mother in the Dordogne. Vanessa, the elder, comes to spend
holidays with them. Laura, is only ten, but her turn will come.

John spent a few years at Forton House School but became
very ill and we had to take him away. He made a slow recovery
over the next few weeks, but the specialist we had consulted
advised no more boarding schools, so some other alternative had
to be found. Grandpa managed to get him into Chard School, at
that time a minor public school with great possibilities, where he
was Chairman of the Board of Governors for several years.

As time went by it became clear John had no intention of following any profession his father might have in mind for him, although he was qualified scholastically well enough to do so. His very varied career included many things, none of which increased his bank balance its true, but certainly helped to develop his character. A talented guitarist with a smooth and delightful style and a voice to match, it's a pity he didn't take it up professionally. He had no encouragement from Grandpa, who made him practice in the potting shed at the far end of the garden. This didn't help him much but his talent isn't wasted as he often plays with a small group at various functions.

Jill lived for a while in a lovely cottage in the glorious countryside of Oxfordshire, just outside Witney, with her three lovable little white West Highland terriers to whom she is so devoted. Lately she has moved to a lovely house in the delightful village of Great Rollright near Chipping Norton where she is very content.

Jocelyn and Sandy after three years in Edinburgh moved to Guernsey. Sandy's most splendid career in the Army resulted in a knighthood and when he retired in 1985 he became Governor of Guernsey.

1984, was a terrible mixture of sadness and change. Grandpa, physically quite spent, died on April 3rd. At almost eighty four I knew I couldn't expect to keep him much longer. His presence is still strongly with us. A vital character such as his will never fade. I feel sure he wouldn't approve of much we do. I really miss his vigorous explosions, arguments and eccentricities as I always knew I would.

When Grandpa was taken ill, I managed to cope for a week on my own but then phoned Jill to come and be with me. She came at once — complete with three dogs and one tortoise — and was a great support for the final few days. She and John took Grandpa to hospital where he was well looked after. We visited him daily but he passed away after one week. Jocelyn was quite unaware of all this as she was in Hong Kong, but eventually we had to phone her with the distressing news.

Jill stayed on until everything was cleared up coping with everything, making all the arrangements, doing all the sorting out and packing for my move to a bungalow. She was often up till gone midnight washing, ironing and polishing. I can never be grateful enough for all she did for me when I was at my lowest. Finally she took me back to Oxfordshire and looked after me until I was able to cope with life again.

Leaving Passlands in John and Mary's care, I've found

myself a little home in the village of Tatworth only a mile or so
outside Chard where I just couldn't be more content. John and
Mary give me help, advice and company and I just couldn't have
moved into my bungalow without them.

I will never know why I've got three such wonderful
children and such a wonderful daughter in law. My dearest hope
is that all my many descendants will be as loving and caring to
their parents as my children are to me.

It is now 1991, and much has happened in the family since I
began this. The best thing, the enormous success John and Mary
are making of their lives, with a very thriving joint venture that
has turned out to be a most remarkable and lucrative business, at
which they both work hard and enthusiastically, enjoying their
work.

Of course I am very fortunate in having many lovely
grandchildren. Jill has provided me with four — Roger, Eve,
Caroline and Nick. Jocelyn and Sandy have gone one better with
no less than five splendid sons — Leslie, Lorne, Lindsay, Lyall
and Louis. John has two daughters of his own from his previous
marriage, Vanessa and Laura, who live in the Dordogne but who
visit him occasionally, as well as four stepchildren — Andrew,
Verity, Chantal, and Gerard.

How fortunate I am to have so many descendants all of
whom I love dearly. Now, I even have some great grandchildren!
Perhaps one day they will read this book to discover something
of their ancestry. I do so hope they will.

Postscript

Since I began writing this, four years have passed and I am now over eighty. Each year seems more wonderfully full than the last. Why is this? Well, I specially want all my descendants to know the reason.

It can be summed up in a single word. Spiritualism. I've always been a seeker after the truth, anything that lacks positive proof is of no use to me. In my early married life, in the Navy, church going was a virtually compulsory performance with which I had to go along. But I did feel a guilty hypocrite as this routine display of man-made ritual, cant and ceremony meant absolutely nothing to me. I was merely conforming to a set of rules that indicated respectability that had nothing whatever to do with spiritual matters. What all the knee bending, hymn singing, standing up and sitting down had to do with where we go and what happens to us when we leave this world was a complete mystery to me. Faith, we are told! Have faith! Oh, yes, I've always had plenty of that. But I wanted proof, some good solid proof to add to it, and now, at last, I've got it.

The knowledge of psychic power enables spiritualists to understand the Bible and its so-called miracles, which Jesus demonstrated, and which are still reproduced by good mediums today. Jesus chose his disciples solely for their psychic power which he knew that, added to his own, would enable him to demonstrate remarkable manifestations such as healing,

179

"Grandma". Daisy Carlene Pomfret neé Blundstone — b. 22nd March 1908. A Dorothy Wilding Studio Photograph taken in London in 1945 when aged 37.

clairvoyance, transfiguration, direct voice, levitation and the crowning glory of his life, materialisation — i.e. the Resurrection!

Some of my very dear friends seem unable to grasp the wonderful truths which are amply illustrated in the Bible, the very book they lay so much store by! However, the younger generation are showing signs of questioning traditional beliefs in their search for spiritual knowledge. They should be encouraged and not made to feel guilty because they question long established man-made beliefs. I am delighted to notice that some of my grandchildren have developed a deep interest and considerable knowledge of the subject without any influence of mine. In mid-summer of 1985 I booked a sitting with a world famous medium, David Young, and on telling my great friend Wal Townsend, he immediately exclaimed, "You just could not have found a better clairvoyant medium". My very dear daughter Jocelyn took me to London to keep my appointment with the medium who knew absolutely nothing about me, not even my name or address! I was merely a number in his appointment book.

What followed, even now four years later, is beyond description. The messages he gave me from Grandpa were completely evidential and so deeply poignant as to bring me to the verge of tears. Some of Grandpa's conversation, relayed to me through David, were of things that were utterly unknown to another soul! Grandpa's personality hadn't changed a scrap, revealing well-known characteristics including some of his choice vocabulary — for which the medium apologised and explained that my husband used the words often when on earth!

I'm leaving my most treasured possession to my dear, much loved, only son, and these are my tape recordings which supply the ultimate proof, with my own voice actually talking, laughing, arguing with Mickey, the little ten year old pert cockney paper boy who was killed crossing a London street over fifty years ago, and who for many many years has been (and still is) the control, for Leslie Flint, the most remarkable and wonderful person ever to come into my life, the Direct Voice Medium, and although I had to wait until I was seventy nine to meet him, it was well worth the wait.

"Nothing happens merely by chance", I consider is the truest statement ever uttered. Through my delightful spiritualist friends, and one in particular, it was arranged and I was able to attend one of Mr. Flint's seances. The word "seance" conjures up weird goings on, but if anyone can call a group of about ten people plus the medium, all talking, laughing, joking with each other, waiting for the voices from beyond to come through and join in, well then this is a "seance". All the proceedings were taped, always; hence my own stock of some wonderful meetings. Whenever I play my tapes I sit stunned all over again!

Many years after I will have happily joined all these wonderful friends and loved ones in the spirit world, (and they all sound as if they are having a real ball) my descendants, some yet to be born, will be able to hear their great, great grandmother's lively repartee with Mickey.

Of course I've got lots and lots of other treasured tapes, which I never get tired of hearing over and over again. Some of the people are tremendously humourous, and they come from all walks of life: from great philosophers, rag and bone men, to clergymen all desperately wanting to come and tell us they are well, happy, fully occupied and very very solidly alive! The latter I might add, reveal a great change of opinion and view point, from the one they taught on earth, confessing they are now much enlightened; now, they are all lovely people, and each one does his utmost to assure us, if only we could but understand, that we should never, never have a second thought about so called "dying" as there is no such thing! Like the idea or not!

All we have to concentrate on is how we live our life here, the love, kindness, and compassion we show our fellow creatures, animals included. No judgment day awaits us, that is a biblical myth, (one of many) as we judge ourselves, we shall find awaiting us exactly what we have put into this life, be it good or evil, and the latter escape nothing, for the law of Karma actually means cause and effect, "As a man sows, so will he reap." This is what in my deepest thoughts always struck me as the truth. Nothing else matters, and in other words it is pure, simple, love of God, His law which can never be broken, and it has another name! *LIFE.*

Among my very precious tape recordings I have one in particular that is especially revealing. A wise and highly evolved guide from Spiritside is being questioned by those on this side about what exactly does happen when we go over there first. The questions were, "We know you volunteered and are trained to help those from earth who come over to your side, do you ever find any difficulty with any of them? "Yes", he replied, "The most difficult ones are those who come over here with fixed, rigid and firm ideas on their orthodox religion". "What do you do with them", was the next question. "Nothing", replied the guide! "They simply join up quite happily with all their friends and loved ones who hold the same opinions. They proceed contentedly with their church-going, festivals and communion rituals, but we can't of course, help them to progress. After a time when they begin to realise that this is getting them nowhere, and when they now and then meet souls who have come from higher spheres they begin to ask 'why can't we go and see and experience these wonders'. It is then we gently explain matters and they then begin to learn the truth, and we can help them." The next question asked from earthside was, "What do you do with atheists who believe nothing at all!" "Oh", said the guide, "they are much easier for us, and make progress faster, because they have nothing to unlearn!"

When I listen to this tape it never fails to touch me deeply, the gentle wisdom and patience of those on the Spiritside towards those whose attitudes on this side, are allowed to be carried over without any correction from anyone, and not until they begin to show signs of enlightenment, can anyone attempt to help them to progress. No pressure at all is used, no persuasion. Think of the multitudes caught up in this web of ignorance, but they never remain for ever in this sad state, mercifully, and once they show any inclination to learn then they get every assistance, but until then, they remain in their "Vale of Delusion" as it is called on Spiritside.

Bear with me just a little longer, no not you who are still on earth and know me, but those dear ones who will never know me, who are yet to be born. Don't get the depressing idea I live from day to day wishing to be gone! Depression is something I don't know the meaning of, I've explained why. I shall be sad to leave my children and those whom I love on this side. I have begged them to think of *me*, not of themselves. They always wanted the best for me, bless them, and surely they must be aware that now, I have got it! I shall be free, free of all the inevitable aches and pains and limitations that old age always brings.

Since completing the book I have, with the full agreement of my family, made arrangements to donate my body for medical research.

My most treasured books and tapes will be in John's keeping. I've asked him to look after them well, and he say's he will. The only sadness I ever feel now is when I hear of friends passing away and I can't go to their relatives and exclaim: "Oh, how happy I am for her, how truly wonderful she must be feeling." I imagine the queer looks I'd get unless of course they, too, are Spiritualists.

I'm never without my nose in a book and my inexhaustable librarian, Wal Townsend, keeps me well supplied, his wisdom on this subject is second to none. Our weekly discussions deepened, increasing my knowledge of Life after Death and its philosophy as Wal unfolded his learning of the subject. I now fully understand that all my past convictions were absolutely right — the Bible, for instance, I now see in a totally different light! It had needed this key of psychic understanding before all doors on anything related to Life after Death could be opened.

Eventually my enthusiasm developed into an ambition which Wal readily shared to form a society to teach these spiritual truths, and which we named THE CHARD PSYCHIC DEBATING SOCIETY. This society is thriving and expanding beyond our expectations as we rapidly become known throughout the spiritualist world. Our meetings attract mediums and speakers of national repute, including those of a scientific approach in other countries and interested in the subject.

In conclusion it might be interesting to mention that Wal and I came together through Wal happening to pick up a copy of Psychic News that contained a letter from me totally denouncing reincarnation! This struck an immediate chord in Wal who contacted me with the result that so much that followed stemmed from that one incident.

I will now quote an impressive passage from a book I am now reading: "Dr. Norman Maclean, the great divine, ex Moderator of the Church of Scotland, bold champion of afflicted, Jewry, made a challenging declaration after one of the many public reunions with the 'war dead' at the Usher Hall, Edinburgh. He it was, who shocked Orthodoxy a few years ago, by admitting it was not until he enquired into Spiritualism that he could understand the Resurrection. 'The church', he quotes, 'whenever it is awake, must welcome this new revelation'." People are demanding to know the truth, and it is impossible any longer to put the enquirers off. Life on this side should be lived to the full, always remembering that what we put into it, is exactly what we can expect to receive on the other side. Whatever we sow, we reap, simply that.

I like to think that what I have written will give my greatly loved and widespread family, a chance to trace their relatives, long after I have departed for those wonderful and happy spheres where I know my many loved ones await me.

March 1991   *Carlene Pomfret*